Praise for

"*Wake Up in Love* flips y~~~ ~~~~~~ ~ practical and Self-inquiry sexy. A personal tale of universal truth, Penelope Love's story evokes feelings we can all resonate with. Weaving poetry and prose in rhythm with the memories of youthful love and childhood scarring, she reveals, identifies, and courageously confronts those internal voices of judgement who haunt through fear and are always wrestling to control the 'I.' This memoir exposes these thoughts for the lies they are, as well as the great teachers they are. Her sharing teaches through example: it is inspiring, infectious, and all the while gently invites us to join her in doing the same."

—RANDAL LYONS, Doctor of Oriental Medicine
Author of *Opening the Eyes of the Heart*

"More than a memoir, this manifesto for authentic non-dual relationship is in essence a contemplation on Love after love. It traces the ambivalent conditioning associated with being raised as a girl in a conventional 1980s Irish- and Italian-Catholic family, the trauma of childhood sexual abuse, her high-achieving disposition at school, the emotional roller coaster of a budding young adult sexuality, a deeply unsatisfactory first marriage, a serendipitous encounter with her spiritual teacher and soon-to-be husband, and her eventual final liberation into Love."

—ÁINE KEENAN, Author of *The Secret: A Contemplation on the Nature of Identity, Reality and Mystery*

"With beautiful language and rare insights, *Wake Up in Love* offers us a thoughtful way to be in relationship with ourselves and others. Penelope Love's brave honesty about intimate details of her human experience is a balm for the tender moments of our own journeys. This is a refreshingly unique message unlike anything I've ever read before. I am grateful for this tribute to love and to a woman courageous enough to live it and share it with us."

—CARRIE SCHMITT, Artist and Author

Praise for WAKE UP IN LOVE

"Emulating Penelope Love's amazing spiritual insight, is it possible? In this memoir, she gives tools to do that very thing—find your authentic Self. As she peels back layers of her thoughts, she couples it with a sometimes painful examination of her childhood, early marriage, and a year of young adult abandoned living. Through this, she meets the 'Who' within and the powerful grace that is her grounding force. Her skill in expressing these deep reflections with poems and prose spurs the reader to recognize, 'I do that, too,' or 'I am like that.' Hence, you come away truer to your own 'I am' within."

—PASTOR MARJORIE WEISS
Author of *Praying on Empty: A Female Pastor's Story*

"Each page of *Wake Up in Love* is a tribute not only to bravery but devotion to what is true and letting go of what is not, of pushing beyond what is known in order to find what is home, and never wavering from the spiritual path. Penelope Love shares so honestly of the hurt and the beauty, the sadness and the joy of the human experience, bringing us into some of the most private and painful places in order to gift us with the possibility of freedom."

—DAPHNE COHN
Writer and Host of the BEYOND Podcast

"In this page-turner, Penelope Love has devoted tremendous energy to bottling her spiritual process that expresses the heart-centered leader within. *Wake Up in Love* taps our inner strength to believe in ourselves and renounce that which doubts us, criticizes our choices, and denies our abilities. This invites us to draw from our reservoir of courage to stand up for what we want most in life. "

—JOHN DICICCO, PHD, Professor, Senior Lecturer, Author of *The Leadership Gene* and Host of the *Leadership is a Choice* Podcast

WAKE UP IN LOVE

A Memoir

Penelope Love

Published in the United States by Open Heart Publishing, a division of Open Heart, LLC, Brasstown, North Carolina.

This is a work of nonfiction. Nonetheless, some names, identifying details, and personal characteristics of the individuals involved have been changed. In addition certain people who appear in these pages are composites of a number of individuals and their experiences. The author of this book does not dispense medical advice or prescribe the use of any technique as a form of treatment for physical, emotional, or medical problems without the advice of a physician, either directly or indirectly. The intent of the author is only to offer information of a general nature to help you in your quest for well-being. In the event you use any of the information in the book for yourself, which is your constitutional right, the author and publisher assume no responsibility for your actions.

Grateful acknowledgment to Nick Gancitano, cover portrait photographer, Dave Fine and Raven Solsong, publishers of early versions of several chapters, and Emily Rodavich for permission to reprint the essay "Fate, Dates and Automobiles," originally published in *Mystical Interludes II*.

Library of Congress Cataloging-in-Publication Data

Love, Penelope
Wake Up in Love: A Memoir

p. cm.
Hardcover ISBN: 978-1-954569-06-5
Paperback ISBN: 978-1-954569-11-9
Ebook ISBN: 978-1-954569-31-7
Library of Congress Control Number: 2021901021
First Trade Paperback Edition, January 2021

For information about special discounts for group purchases, please call +1-828-237-2555 or email Sales@OpenHeartPublishing.com.

"Be true! Be true! Be true!
Show freely to the world,
if not your worst,
yet some trait whereby
the worst may be inferred!"

—Nathaniel Hawthorne

Contents

Contents ... Continued

Poetry

Love Is

Love is a path

of unwinding Grace,

an infinite journey

to the nearest

space

PREFACE

By my late twenties, I had acquired everything I was taught to want: a master's degree, a blossoming career, a curvaceous body, a sporty car, a handsome hubby, and an address in a lavish Palm Beach polo club. Yet, instead of leaping out of bed in the morning, I barely had the will to pull the sheets down from over my head. My then-husband and I existed on split schedules. At dawn, I dashed off on my commute while he lay fast asleep. Nine hours later, my attempts to rekindle passion via candlelit dinners were thwarted by an alarm that meant only one thing: his business calls with China were just beginning. As I dined alone with my girlfriends on speaker, I dared not reveal my fairytale life was a facade, resorting instead to the antidepressants that sustained this former homecoming queen.

The illusion could not go on. Following our separation, nine months of psychotherapy, three prescription refills, and five relationship attempts with other men while awaiting legal confirmation of my divorce, I was led to a meditation class by the echoed urgings of my therapist, a lover, and a slew of self-help authors at the publishing company where I worked. Immediately I experienced some basic benefits of meditation: I was breathing more deeply and catching thoughts before they coalesced into a menagerie of mental mayhem. I felt less anxious and the proof shined through my eyes.

"It is so peaceful in your office," a colleague said. "What's up?"

"I'm meditating and practicing Self-inquiry," I replied. "Some of this stuff we publish books about, it really works!"

And *poof!* My reputation as the distressed editor of *Counselor* magazine was no more.

"I am also in love," I confessed.

Ever a romantic, I'd fallen instantly in love with my spiritual teacher. This time I *knew* it was different. Accessing deep states of inner peace had become my priority and thoughts of sex and romance had temporarily dissolved into the desire to know supreme peace. I was a sponge for learning meditation, which I found out was not about watching thoughts but fixing my attention on *one idea* to the exclusion of all other thoughts. The added practice of Self-inquiry: fixing my attention on my Self-as-pure-awareness, making my Self that one *"idea,"* quickly stripped away the inner critic that once ridiculed me for crushing on my instructors. Blessed I was this time, as my desires to meditate and to find love converged when I met this man. The recognition of our karmic connection was instantaneous and we'd marry within two weeks!

Without knowing it, I'd done something unthinkable in spiritual circles: I'd become intimately involved with my "guru." Apparently this was a categorical no-no, but it was too late. At that point in my life, I'd never heard or read anything about the abuses of power within certain spiritual organizations. It is *essential* to question the dynamics at play in any relationship and I did. Over the years, concern had been raised by some but was quickly abandoned by those who spent more than a few moments with us. The question of whether our relationship was ethical disappeared in the light of my direct experience and clear signs that we were meant to be together.

During the first few months of our marriage, my life turned inside out. I moved out of my bachelorette pad and into Atma-Vichara Ashram, a spiritual training center in Florida where many other students lived communally. A daily seated practice beginning at 5:30 a.m., enhanced by various active meditations throughout the day, strengthened my connection with God, which released me from any dependency I had on antidepressants. From there, I grew in confidence to speak my truth to my bosses and co-workers and did so even when I sensed my opinion was not going to be tolerated by the majority, a prelude to my exit from the corporate world. I also stood up to my disapproving family in ways I never believed possible, taking charge of my own life decisions and not allowing their opinions to influence my experience of the spiritual family I was discovering. Meanwhile, the marriage of meditation and sexuality was literally rocking my world. Daily lovemaking was unfolding as a practice of the ancient art of Tantra, through which I began to experience profound emotional healing of sexual trauma buried in the darkest recesses of my subconscious. Whether cradled in my lover's arms or absorbed in the day's activities, I felt the embrace of God's grace. I felt *alive!*

Exactly six months after my first class, I found myself meditating in Virupaksha Cave on the sacred hill of Arunachala in Tiruvannamalai, India. Yes, marrying a conscious teacher had fortified my resolve to be still, yet never would I have imagined myself dredging up the courage to close my eyes in a dark cave that I had to literally crawl into. After all, I had only just parted with my mace key chain. So caught up had I been in the fear of nearly everything, I suppose I had to wind up in a hole on the other side of the earth to finally acknowledge that life was becoming very different now.

Following six weeks in India, I returned to Florida jobless, started my own business as a freelance editor, and remained devoted to my daily regimen. It now included three hours of seated meditation, plus selfless service, spiritual reading, sacred lovemaking, and conscious day-planning via what I affectionately call

"The Holy Sheets." Filled out every evening, these sheets were designed to document upset patterns, insights, and unfinished communications to be completed before bedtime. My partner, my housemates, and the sheets held me accountable for everything I once resisted, especially when my tendency to project and blame others threatened my only chance for true happiness.

When I returned to India the following year, the life I'd struggled desperately to hold onto as "mine" underwent an irreversible paradigm shift in consciousness. More than fifteen months of living in close quarters with my spiritual family, each confronting our issues about food, sex, and money in a living workshop, had challenged my conditioning of seeing the world as a solid reality that I once considered "my life."

On Christmas morning spent in silence on Arunachala, the insight culminated in a heated process, with my partner challenging my notion of "the real world" as well as the idea that I existed in it merely as a separate and unique snowflake or person. As my limbs trembled, "Life, as I've known it, is over!" rolled off my tongue. Not a moment later, the thought *I don't want it to be over!* retaliated. My body collapsed in tears and laughter; an awakening transpired while I lay in his embrace. With no thought of "me" to be found, nor a story to attach it to, I fell inward, remembering my True Nature in a manner that It could not be forgotten.

Fundamentally my spiritual practice blended Self-inquiry and Tantra. Misunderstanding of Tantra runs rampant in modern culture, which emphasizes its sexual component to the exclusion of its less titillating but no less essential foundation of Self-awareness. My service to humanity as such is to help resolve any confusion those awakening may have about it and to certify that Tantra is more than a novel approach to sex: it is a full embrace of life that untangles the human predicament through conscious exploration of desire, taking normally unconscious, body-centric processes, including eating and sex, and transforms them into meditations. The potent combination of Tantra and Self-inquiry yields the embodiment of Self-awareness, where one senses their essential unity with the Creator and all existence.

As my heart opened to oneness, my late German grandfather appeared three times in different dreams, pointing to the light of Christ and offering a simple blessing: "Be happy." Meanwhile in the earthly realm, my conventional Irish- and Italian-Catholic family of origin vehemently opposed my new marriage. They disparaged my husband as "the guru" without ever meeting him, bearing witness to our love, or experiencing Self-inquiry and the ashram themselves. The parents' voicemails and emails made it clear they were *none too pleased* that I had taken up meditation and communal living, never mind Tantra (which I made the faux pas of trying to explain to my mother). Their unfounded statements further incited my inner rebel, and overnight their docile little lamb transformed into the black sheep of the family. All attempts to manipulate my behavior failed in vain—they had completely lost control of "their daughter"!

To suggest my life choices were unacceptable to them is an understatement. One day while waiting for my computer to be repaired at the Apple Store Genius Bar, I checked my email on one of the showroom computers only to find, buried in a stack of love-mail from my sweetheart, a diatribe about how my decision to marry "the guru" and live communally had forever shamed me in the eyes of the family, the world, and—yes—God! It was signed "Love, Grandma," but I sensed that this matriarchal message spoke for the entire family.

In that moment, the deep-seated fear of exile swelled in my cells. I began to sob, but what drew everyone's attention was the *"oh, fuck"* that escaped my lips. While I was choking on snot, a legion of tech-support heroes approached to ask if I was okay. I couldn't speak as I teetered on the edge of either going back to my old life

or realizing that I didn't have to conform to my family's beliefs
about what was best for me, or any other beliefs for that matter.

In this moment of reckoning, no words uttered by my Romeo
or a well-meaning Genius could console me. But it was okay. My
Soul was speaking within me: *I choose love. I choose truth. I Am love.
I Am truth.* This inner knowing set in as I saw the Apple logo—with
the little bite out of it—flashing everywhere. Now I understood:
in my family's eyes, I had eaten the forbidden fruit, but through my
own body I had tasted God's presence and life was bursting with
health and deliciousness! Shortly thereafter I left the mall hand-
in-hand with my husband, with much more than my laptop fixed.

After an evening of deep deliberation, I did not reply to my
grandmother's email. Instead I turned to my trusty journal, wherein
I came to appreciate her perspective as that of a conservative
Catholic who was caring about her granddaughter the only way
she knew how. Perhaps for her the commandment to honor thy
father and mother meant to obey them and live according to their
wishes. *But did honor necessarily mean obey?* Certainly not blindly.
Yet I appreciated that my grandmother's penchant for writing,
literature, and D.H. Lawrence in particular, had influenced me
tremendously. Nearly a century after his death, his pet themes are
canonized as "freedom, redemption, the difficulty and necessity
of emotional and erotic expression, and the inevitable torments
of family relationships."[1]

> *Is this anguish inevitable?*
> *Will my family ever accept me as I am?*
> *If they don't, what then?*

> Only God could have scripted this crazy dream.
> It was obvious . . . the only way out was in.
> I had to wake up.

So I Would Wake Up

Forgive me
for I knew not what I did
when in my flesh and bones
You hid
sounding the alarms
shame, blame, pain and fear
so I'd wake up
in Your loving arms —
Right Here

INTRODUCTION

$\mathcal{W}$aking up in love, a.k.a. spiritual awakening through relationship, never happens by accident. Instead it occurs in the coupling of lovers who intentionally harness the power of intimacy, in essence allowing their body and mind to function as each other's *guru* (and let's define guru not as a person but as *a function of God's grace acting to dissolve all sense of separation*). This awakening is a long-intended journey of the soul that comes to realize its true Self shining first through one's lover and eventually through all. Not everyone is on this path of spiritual awakening, yet those who harbor this sacred desire to wake up in love may have found themselves, like yours truly, obsessed with finding "true love" since childhood.

Ever since I could read fairy tales, I imagined that someone else could affirm the worth of my existence and make me happy once and for all. Today I chuckle at how virtually every man I'd ever met became a viable candidate for my prince charming. My relationships with every male classmate, teacher, coach, professor, or you name it, were just an agonizing process of feeling my "hooks" tear into these poor guys at first sight.

I was twenty-eight when I finally declawed myself. Declining a friend's invite to Friday night happy hour, I chose the solitude of my bachelorette pad. I ended up sprawled on my bed, sobbing into a silky orange pillow and gasping for breath between paragraphs of Debbie Ford's *Spiritual Divorce*. At one point, I put down the book to stare at my Blackberry screen full of sexts from my latest boy toy. There alone with my phone, my heart sank, but I also felt something deeper emerging. It was the first time I remembered to ask God for help when I felt desperate. I rolled off the bed, got down on my knees, and I prayed:

> *Please show me how to find inner peace, just like all the teachers in the Sounds True catalog. Please release me from the sob story about how I cannot find a man. Please help me fall asleep without crying tonight. Please help me appreciate feeling these soft sheets all over my body rather than brooding over who's not in bed with me. Please let me sleep through the night. Please help me get through the weekend. Please make sure I show up for meditation class Tuesday. And please help me get off these damn antidepressants. Thank you. Amen.*

The prayer was answered because from Saturday to Monday, I went about my daily activities in peace. Rather than downing day-old coffee and a glob of peanut butter on toast, I ate fruit for breakfast and drank tea. I finally unwrapped a Shiva Rea yoga CD I'd purchased months earlier. I closed my eyes and flowed according to her instructions, completing the class without worrying that I couldn't reach my toes. I treated myself to a Swedish massage and splurged on another CD, one of Sanskrit chants that had been playing in the background while a strong, lovely Indian woman worked the knots out of my aching body. For the rest of the weekend, I let those mantras play on a loop. I had no idea what the chants meant, but I felt the music and the mantras radiating comfort through my being. Immersed in all of these higher vibrations, I stopped expecting *him* to appear.

Yet on Tuesday . . . he did!

∞

Ever since my first day on the job in the self-help publishing industry, I'd felt myself drowning in the ocean of other people's advice. But within a few weeks of meditating daily, my inner compass became balanced enough to distinguish unconscious babble from the inner voice of direct insight. I felt reborn and *knew* I needed a new name, first and last. My divorce already had me considering the implications of taking back my birth name, but it no longer fit. Before legally changing my name, a spiritual process described in Part One, I simply asked people to call me Penelope Love. From Masaru Emoto's experiments with water crystals featured in the documentary *What the Bleep Do We Know?*,[2] I understood enough about vibration to know that words do matter. And if I wanted to know Love as my essence, wouldn't naming myself "Love" be the utmost affirmation?

Needless to say, the name change did not go over well with *la famiglia*, but I expected that. What I didn't see coming was the lack of response from most of my colleagues. Because the company published books about personal transformation, I assumed my peers' enthusiasm about my name change would match my own. My boss's seemed to when he encouraged me to send a company-wide email to notify the whole staff. Yet to this day, I can count on one hand the number of my then-coworkers who ever spoke to me again. "I didn't realize you'd changed your last name too" was all my boss said to me for the rest of the day.

The company's editorial director was of a different breed. When he stopped by my office to say "Hello, Penelope!" it sparked a life-changing conversation. A fellow fan of *What the Bleep Do We Know?*, he seemed to understand the urgency of what was at stake. He *got* that I was shedding everything that had been familiar to me, that I was in the cocoon-cracking stage of transcending patterns destructive to body and soul. We talked about some of the books that had inspired my changes, and true to his professional role, he encouraged me to write about my experiences.

Since he was the one who brought up writing, I seized my private moment with this busy department leader and asked, "What makes you publish one book over another?"

I remember his answer practically verbatim.

"A writer must write the book only he or she can write," he said. "That's what makes a book that's unlike any other. That's what makes a book that changes lives."

Over the years, as my career focus shifted from the magazine to books, I observed this too. Through my editor's specs, I watched the Information Age extend a great temptation to quote the words of others, which are all too easy to cut and paste, tweak, and claim as one's own. And this phenomenon was lining bookstore shelves with content that all smelled the same, but wore different, fancy covers. It was true: *only writing from one's own direct experience could catalyze transformation.*

And so I wrote this book over a sixteen-year period, returning repeatedly to this question: *What will it do for you that no other book does?* It provides a fresh perspective on the wisdom I discovered—namely, the timeless tools that not only attract, cultivate and sustain a loving relationship, but also transform sex into the ultimate meditation for the realization of God and perpetual happiness. Applying this wisdom turns not just your relationship but your whole life into a magnificent love affair where you can genuinely say, "Yes, I wake up in love, every day."

The core of this book is the "Love Life" column I wrote for *Montaña al Mar,* a magazine about sustainable living in my former residence of southern Costa Rica. My husband and I lived there for three glorious years. Our cabin, tucked deep within a five-hundred-acre nature preserve, was a mile away from the nearest humans and a two-to-three-hour journey to the nearest city with a grocery store. Still I wrote daily and traveled to town weekly to take Spanish lessons and shop for necessities. In the streets, people would recognize me from my head shot in the magazine. In fact, my memories of the readers' comments and hugs inspired me to write this book.

And so I offer you *Wake Up in Love*. It is a prayer, a celebration of love, and a metaphorical tuning fork. When a tuning fork vibrates, other tuning forks in its proximity begin vibrating at the same frequency. This principle has played out over the years of my marriage with Nick in that people who have spent significant time with us not only have met conscious lovers but even married their soul mate. The message in this book is intended to catalyze your attunement to the vibration of your inner love, to recognize and cherish it in all its forms, to embrace it and not take love for granted, and to help you know this: if your heart desires to wake up in love, then it is your destiny.

Take a Backward Bow

All exploration is preparation

for the moment the wind blows just so —

you forget everything you know

and fall in love

with the endless show

as you take a backward bow

to the miracle of how

The One you've been looking for

finds You

and the exploration begins

anew

PART ONE

Everything Can Prepare You

Love Myself First

To stay in this "marriage" or get divorced?

The heart's decisions are never forced

I knew the choice I had to make

but not the twist the path would take

The false affair paved way for the true

I vowed "love myself first"

and so

I do

Divorcing My Old Ways

*O*nce taboo as the forbidden fruit, divorce turned out to be the seed that cracked my heart open and sprouted a whole new life. Countless nights I'd cried, mascara-staining my pillow while my then-husband slept soundly beside me. I had no foresight of the exquisite journey awaiting me on the other side of our separation. It would lead me back to Eden by way of the pursuit of truth.

Initially when I told people I'd decided to leave my marriage, the usual responses came: "I'm sorry to hear it" or "Too bad it didn't work out." This only intensified my fog of depression. Then one day someone said, "Congratulations!" and it stunned me.

Could divorce actually be a celebration?

Raised Catholic in the '70s and '80s, I wasn't brought up to think it so. I knew some adults who refrained from receiving Holy Communion at church because they were divorced. The way I understood it, certain sins were forgivable through penance but in most cases divorce was not one of those. Even though I was not an active churchgoer when my marriage ended, I still glorified the "Romantic" Catholic notion of "until death do us part," and deep in my bones I feared eternal damnation from breaking those wedding vows.

Yet times had changed between the '70s and the new millennium. In 1969, California initiated the trend of U.S. states adopting no-fault divorce laws permitting a mere declaration of "irreconcilable differences" as grounds for divorce. Outside of church, divorce was not as taboo as my religious conditioning indicated. This contradiction caused me to wrestle with my beliefs. In one light, I was "sinning" and in the same breath I felt the support of counselors, friends, and unhappily married family members who encouraged me to pursue happiness and well-being, with the chance of future love.

Did I deserve love?

And could I ever get married again?

These questions gnawed at my insides. After confessing them to my therapist, two words shifted everything for me.

"You are a *gute neshome,*" she whispered through my panic while handing me a tissue; then she translated the Yiddish phrase. "You are a *good soul.*" The resonance of *gute neshome* calmed me like a babe at her mother's breast. The ensuing wave of white noise cancelled out the raspy inner critic fighting to convince me I was damaged goods. That two-word lullaby halted all wonderings of what I'd done to cause my then-husband to not want me anymore. The affirmation set me free for a minute. And then my proverbial monkey-mind began swinging between two types of branches: *Was I a good soul or a bad soul?*

I much preferred the shiny, new good-soul I.D. For about a year, I roamed the jungle of society, hunting amongst a slew of alpha males and desperately hoping that, beyond the pheromones, they'd sense the essence of a good soul.

After many lovers, I still cried myself to sleep, alone and confused. This inner conflict catapulted me onto the path of Self-inquiry. With fresh good-soul confidence, I'd attracted lovers but I still wanted them from an empty place of needing them to love me. The inner desperation reeked. It did not drive men wild, it drove them away, leaving me hanging frantically on the bad-soul beliefs again.

As the suffering grew, what else could I do?

I had no choice, no choice except one, but then it wasn't really a choice . . .

I let go.

ABOUT THAT PRINCE...

*O*ne of the first lessons I internalized in life was that a man was going to marry me and rescue me from unimaginable danger, and it could not be my father because God clearly had assigned him to my mother. Yet, God had a son named Jesus who would save me and as my luck would have it, he would be coming back to earth, probably any day now . . . *could he be The One?*

> *Lamb of God, you take away the sins of the world,*
> *have mercy on us.*
>
> *Lamb of God, you take away the sins of the world,*
> *have mercy on us.*
>
> *Lamb of God, you take away the sins of the world,*
> *grant us peace.*

Week after week, I repeated the words but could not figure out what they meant, despite attending CCD and Sunday mass, my bony hand squirming in my mother's as I sat, lips sealed, and ears open to the deep rumble of a priest I couldn't comprehend.

All of the standing and genuflecting provided relief from leg stiffness born of the wooden pew, and the music a chance to sway and sing along with songs I came to know. But the lyrics, they raised perplexing questions too. Chills ascended my spine every time the congregation sang my favorite hymn, *Here I Am, Lord,* all of us asking in powerful unison, "Is it I, Lord?"

Why that question? Who was I in relationship to God? And why was I here? When I tapped my mother's knee and started to ask her once, our pew neighbors' *shhhhh!* response branded my cheeks red with the fire of shame. Apparently church was not a place for questions.

At least my eyes were free to roam and roam they did, from dust particle to dust particle in the light streaming through the high arches and stained-glass windows. Before long, my gaze would settle on the mosaic of a crucified Jesus Christ, INRI posted over his limp and tortured corpse, *Iesus Nazarenus Rex Iudaeorum,* King of the Jews.

Why on earth would anyone have hurt him like this, driving stakes through his wrists and feet, and a crown of thorns into his skull, a beloved man we call the Prince of Peace?

I kept my lips sealed and never asked, having learned early that children, especially daughters of Sicilian fathers, were meant to be seen and not heard. I'd witnessed the teacher's scolding of my CCD classmate Bobby, who bore a striking resemblance to Dennis the Menace as he challenged her. I knew the sting of my father's belt that awaited me if I were to dare pull a Bobby. What else could I do but develop a crush on this brave boy whose same unanswered questions remained stuck in my throat?

Years later, in my OCD-driven teens, my thoughts became so twisted that I actually thought it possible Jesus had died because of my sins, especially my lust after boys. Yes, my behavior two thousand years later would be so atrocious that he had to die way back then because of the unspeakable things I would do, not to mention all of the *meow,* wild things I wanted to do. In which case, it was likely that Jesus decided he would rather not witness the aftermath of my forays into Barnes & Noble's Kama Sutra section and my clandestine camouflaging of glossy sex manuals between the covers of the *Barron's SAT* prep manual to hide the material I was actually studying.

I confess that, in my university years, I attended mass on campus more as a social activity than a religious practice. *Why miss a chance of being picked up by a good Catholic man who would whisk me to the altar and into the sacred sack?* At that point, I was a loyal subscriber to the no-sex-before-marriage list, which meant all of the energy that would have been otherwise released in sexual escapades was ricocheting in my brain. The more I heard the priest say, "Jesus died for your sins," the more I started to consider possible alternative meanings for the phrase. These theories were undoubtedly influenced by my venture into Women's Studies. Maybe it was meant in the sense that he'd died so that I could sin liberally, in which case I could do *whatever* and then proceed to the line of human souls begging for forgiveness at the gates of heaven. Or, was it all just some big conspiracy to trick me into good behavior? *Hmmm?*

None of my bizarro theories resonated with the love I felt when I meditated on the presence of Jesus the Christ. At various points in my metamorphosis from child to woman, when I asked my mother, "How could one man take on the sins of the entire world?" she would say that she didn't know how, that's just the way it was. And each time I thought, *Wow, I couldn't be capable of such a courageous and selfless feat.*

From then on, it was decided: *That's what men are supposed to do—like Jesus, they are supposed to save me, so I don't have to suffer. Well, sounds good to me!*

In my youth, I turned to my younger brother in times of emotional turmoil. I always felt he saved my life by cutting the pain of living in half, with our father's hostility spilt between two of us instead of focused all on yours truly. As a team, my brother and I were so adept at guarding our own lives, in our teens we found summer employment as lifeguards.

Once I was treading water beneath the diving board, waiting for a long line of beginner swimmers to jump into the half-circle between my open arms and doggie-paddle themselves to the ladder. When an extra-large tween jumped onto my head instead, the world went black. Next thing I knew, a massive surge of power from beneath was lifting me upward with the force of a dolphin. When we broke surface, my eyes popped open to the sight of my brother carrying me and the XL newbie to safety.

Then there was my second-generation Sicilian father, whose bullying all but demanded I consider him my savior. "Who brings home the bacon? Who puts clothes on your back and shoes on your feet and a fuckin' roof over your head? Who pays for your piano lessons?" Whenever he spat out these questions, I wanted to scream. Yes, there were tender times that his gruff edges softened as he rescued me from trouble, like in seventh grade, when my friends and I had prank-called a Chinese restaurant enough times that the police came to our home to arrest me as a juvenile (he smoothed things over with the officers, whom he knew from a telephone installation job he'd done at the police station) but I digress. Somehow my father's actions, no matter his motives, only reinforced my belief that men were forceful and therefore stronger, and thus women needed to be submissive so that men would save them.

Fast-forward two decades since my father had saved me from juvenile prison. I got caught up in a fling with a man from work, a PR agent who used to call regularly and pitch articles to the magazine. This 6' 8" gent with an über-sexy voice bought me a black leather journal, but it was not for drafting my "From the Editor" column. He encouraged me to write about my inner life, my heart's desires, to just let it rip. From time to time, he would ask me if I wanted to read him my intimate scribblings, which of course I did. Then he'd tell me they were "pretty good" but I could do better ... that he wanted to see me naked on the page. So I stripped in words, and in body, but never received praise or a diamond ring. *Where had I failed? What was wrong with me?*

One night after this man and I hung up from our final phone call, a few days after I had met my beloved teacher, I busted out that tattered journal and spilled new wisdom across the page:

"Bastard said I'm not over him yet or I wouldn't have had to call him to convince him that I was. Dammit, he is right. And then he has the nerve to accuse me of looking for a man to save me! Wait, am I?"

It's time to let go of the idea that you need saving.

Love,
God

"I didn't realize that I'd even thought that!"

Whoa. I set the journal down to let that simmer. Later, my heart poured through my pen:

No one is going to save you because there is no one else to do the saving, no one to be saved from, and ultimately, no one to be saved.

"Wait! What about Mary Magdalene? Wasn't she also searching for a savior?" I scribbled furiously.

No. Mary Magdalene, after long-suffering, was confronted with the unconditional love of Jesus and His forgiveness. So ripe was her desire for truth that "when the disciple is ready, the master will appear." Yet, what matters is the key her story holds for you now.

"Go on, please..."

The key to unlocking humility in your heart is to acknowledge you are suffering. You cannot progress without first accepting this fact. Your problem has been your pride: you want the world to think you've got it all together. You sing along with the famous song but you don't dare admit, "I Don't Know How to Love Him." You don't divulge to even your closest friends that your private life is in shambles, because you perceive that theirs are better, and you strive to win that losing game called comparison. If you want to be happy, stop it now! Be honest. Be vulnerable. Be not afraid. Meet the pain of life head on, heart open. This is the only way to love.

Go ahead, kiss ten thousand frogs if you enjoy that, but not one is morphing into a prince who is going to save you... look within. Who is there to be saved?

"Me," you say. But who is looking?

"I am," you say.

But who is this "I" seeing "me" from within?

This "me" you've dreamed yourself to be must get hurt for one reason alone: to realize You can never be hurt. And if you ever forget it, even for a moment, simply investigate "Who am I?" and you shall know the truth.

My New Man-tra

May I always see the God in men —

the God I Am

Forward Movement

*Y*ou know that relative who forwards you email chain letters like it's 1995? Well, in 2004 (a.k.a. my limbo year between marriages), mine sent me countless jokes about men, no doubt reflecting the resentment I was projecting toward them. But one fateful day, an unfamiliar urge stopped my finger from pressing the forward button too. Instead, I opened a blank document instead, where my inner voice then spoke in 12-point Times New Roman:

> *Hell may hath no fury like a woman scorned, but really, Penelope, what is the price of contempt? Why spread venom? For what purpose?*

Taken aback that such compassion had arisen in me, a woman who believed all men to be like her abusive father, I'd cornered myself into a moment of self-reflection. I had a few more questions for this wise inner part.

"What brings you here, Higher Self?" my fingers typed.

> *Your prayerful desire to fully love a man—in fact, all men. And to realize there is no need to fear them. But let's start with one man, okay?*

Oh my . . . God! It is you! You're the one dancing my hands across this keyboard. Now I'm not exactly Neale Donald Walsch here, so please speak slowly. Thank you. Amen.

Consider the jokes that you've seen running rampant on the Internet. It's true, they contain the potential to perpetuate the hatred of men. Yet therein lies the real joke—because men are not monsters but mirrors within the dream of your life, reflecting qualities you've been conditioned to see in "man," while expressing yourself as a "woman."

What makes men *men*, then?

The collective of "men" is an idea, manifesting in precisely the manner you've imagined them. And so, if you are desiring the men in your life to exhibit different qualities, it is you who must first change.

Oh, like in *The Matrix*, the line about the spoon not bending, only yourself. I get it! I think. No, wait, I don't. So how do I change? I mean, what interior changes can I make to manifest changes in the types of men I attract?

Understand, you do not attract "types" of men. I Am always drawing the beings to you with the most power to evolve you spiritually. It is I who give them that power, out of My love for you. There are no "types." The idea of "types" reflects a categorization of the mind that perpetuates the illusion that "others" even exist, and so these "others" do "appear" to exist in your experience.

In the matrix that is your world, there will always be those characters who categorize people into groups—the jocks, the studs, the nerds, the drunks, the players, the Goths, the Gordon Gekkos, etc. Be wary of such categories, for each being is a unique expression of Me, Your Highest Self, and thus beyond categorization.

So, to answer the heart of your question: You have to be willing to stop. Stop categorizing. Stop judging. Drop the delusion that the mind has fabricated to ensure its continued existence, which clouds the clear vision of who you really are: the infinite consciousness. Do not begrudge the mind; it is just doing its job. We've got to have some live entertainment here! Otherwise, where is life's purpose?

Ultimately, each being is a focal point of My Being. So if you want your categorization to be accurate, you would have to consider infinite categories—which puts us right back where we started from: no meaningful categories. This makes all the men you see . . .

Oh my . . . G-O-D!

That's right. Every single one of them is Me. But before you are ready to see even one man in this light, you must be willing to see yourself in an equally favorable light that reflects your infinite beauty. That's where being still comes in, so get thee to . . .

A nunnery?

No, that won't be necessary. Meditation class will suffice.

WHO FALLS IN LOVE ANYWAY?

*I*n all my then-twenty-eight years, I had not seen it coming—
and if an angel had descended on earth to whisper in my
ear that it would happen, I still would not have believed that *this* is
how I would meet my soul mate.

It was a generic Thursday morning at the office when the
blue-eyed, athletic Ivy League grad I was dating dialed me on my
work phone.

"Sorry to call you at work but there's something important I'd
like to communicate with you," he said.

A guy, wanting to communicate with me? This one's a keeper!

"I'd still love for us to date," he went on, "but I felt it would only
be fair to tell you that I'm planning to date other women too."

Not again, I thought as I buried my face in the palm of my
hand. *Not . . . again!*

But I managed to eke out a few words between my shortening
breaths. "You know I want monogamy, so let's just call it off
altogether."

He must have sensed my panic attack coming on.

"Hey, write down this number," he said. "Wait, I'm not even sure what all of the numbers are . . . it's 954-2**-YOGA."

"Ummmmm, okay," I said, scribbling it down on a hot-pink sticky note.

"You'd definitely benefit from meditation," he said.

So now he's my therapist? I burst into tears.

"Actually, it's more than meditation," he said, "it's *satsang.*"

"Wh, wh, what's *satsang?*" I whimpered.

"It's Sanskrit for gathering in association with a spiritually awakened one," he said. "Another way of translating it is 'conscious company.'"

In between my sobs, he went on to tell me that I could learn to meditate at this local ashram under the guidance and direction of a teacher, his former football coach who now taught something called Self-inquiry. I'd already looked up what the word *ashram* meant, given the number of times he'd used it on our first date. I understood it to be a place to receive spiritual instruction for the intention of evolving consciously, but I'd forgotten about it until he brought it up again.

"You'll love Nick . . . I mean, I Am," he said. "He goes by the name I Am, and you're deep so I just know you're going to get it."

Deep? I thought. *Geez, how deep do I have to be to qualify for monogamy?*

"What does being deep have to do with this?" I asked. "And by 'it' I know you're not talking about sex, so what gives?"

"I can't explain it, you just have to go meet I Am and experience Self-inquiry," he said. "And side note, you guys are both from Coral Springs."

"Ummm, okay," I said again, drying my eyes with a crumpled napkin and regathering composure. "And hey, thanks for letting me know you wanted to sleep with other women and not just doing it."

"You're welcome," he said. "And hey, I really did enjoy our dates." I sat there shaking my head, staring at the number on the sticky note.

"Before I go, is there anything else you would like to communicate with me?" he asked.

So. Weird. What is up with that question?! I thought. *Isn't he the one who called to communicate with ME? And why does he keep saying "communicate"?*

"No, that's all," I said. "Bye now."

Click. He hung up first and as I reached over to hang up too, I noticed the strangest thing—the panic attack symptoms had disappeared.

My second panic attack of the day hit just after the last bite of my tabouleh salad. I'd eaten once again at my desk in the company of my only steady lunch date in those days, an older, slower Windows 98 PC.

I'd been thinking about making this call for hours, and I knew what I needed to do.

Tingles in my arms and chest, I fought the limpness in my fingers as they dialed a co-worker in the IT department. He picked up on the first ring and I whispered my plea so no one else would hear it. "Hey, would you please grab me a book from the basement archives?"

"Sure. Which one do you need?" he asked.

"Uhhh, the one about born-again virginity," I said.

He chuckled, but it was a yes from him. This colleague was the kind of listener I could talk to about anything and often did, so he wasn't surprised.

"Bring it up after hours so no one else will see?" I asked.

He snorted with laughter as I caught a deep breath and . . .

Click. The sound of the handset hitting the phone base sent waves through me. Making this call symbolized my new commitment to myself, yet deep down I knew that speed-reading another book wasn't really going to be the panacea to my heartache. There was one more call I had to make.

Back at my apartment later that evening, with my kitten as a moral support, I called the ashram to reserve my seat at Tuesday's meditation. I'd completely not processed the football-coach part, and my mind's image of a guru—a borderline anorexic-looking, nearly naked guy crowned with a white turban—had taken root in my mind. Over the phone, the voice of this teacher matched that image; it was soft yet strong and just as I'd hoped for, he sounded incredibly wise. I hung up confident that this man, unlike my dusty pile of self-help CDs, could teach me to meditate and find some of that inner peace I'd read so much about, although I'd never seriously practiced any of it myself.

I'd always been the kind of girl who developed crushes on male teachers, devoting excessive hours to perfecting the homework they assigned, in dire need of their approval. So, I'd made a point of telling *I Am* that I was the editor of a major magazine, for which I was planning a feature on meditation. This way, he would be impressed even in advance of my arrival.

Over the next few days, I returned to my natural workaholic state. Tuesday evening rolled around so quickly that I failed to leave work early enough to ensure my prompt arrival at a place I'd never been before. I rushed in, one minute late! Even though I had called from the car to double-check the directions, I knew that being late for a class of this nature implied a lack of respect. Even before arriving there, I'd already committed a cardinal sin of yoga.

It didn't matter: I felt forgiven for every wrong thing I'd ever done in my life the instant I locked eyes with *I Am*. Those warm, golden-brown eyes shined not from beneath a high, twisting turban, but a receding hairline, complimented by a plump face with the smile of a cherub and a belly to match. Sitting there quietly in half lotus, he did not resemble my idea of a man I'd fall in love with.

Right there, in that moment, I realized it is not bodies that fall in love.

Who Is This?

The moment
you looked
in my eyes
I died —
guilt,
pride,
... gone!
I was nothing,
a gaping whole
filled with grace,
beauty without a face
looking into
the nature of
my I's.
I love,
I exist,
and who is this?
I am —
revealing
you to be
nothing
but me
in the end,
now
forever
my best
friend

FATE, DATES AND AUTOMOBILES

*M*y teacher asked me out the day after we met in *satsang* in the summer of 2004. Little did I realize, our love story in this lifetime had already begun.

1992

"*Atten-tion!*" Mr. Womack's military command sliced through the air, dissolving all chatter in the Coral Springs High School hallway adjacent to a trophy case lining the cafeteria entrance. "Form your lines!" he ordered.

My heart pounded as sweat dripped beneath my starched-stiff polyester uniform, foreshadowing the intense Florida heat awaiting us outdoors. I'd tooted countless breaths, arranged my spindly fingers in innumerable positions, and marched a million steps to arrive precisely at this point in space-time. It was my junior year, and I was *the* chick with the pic—the piccolo, that is. I was the section leader of the mighty flutes.

Another bead of sweat fell, then . . . electric silence as I awaited the next marching order.

"Flutes, here!" Mr. Womack pointed to the exact spot I should stand. "Face the wall!"

But this was no ordinary spot on the wall. His order had placed me and the entire flute brigade before the honorary historical portraits of our school's legendary All-State athletes.

At eye level before me hung the photograph of a handsome 1981 All-State soccer player. One step left, it would have been a baseball player—or to the right, a basketball star. One step in either direction would have changed my destiny. I'd been ordered to stare at this precise spot, home to this young man's fading photograph. I never took note of his name, so captivated was I by the cheerful glint in his light-brown eyes, the confident curve of his smile, the '80s-style shortness of his blue soccer shorts, and the sheer size of his muscular thighs, but I digress. Of course, I focused mainly on his eyes.

What a nice boyfriend he'd have been, had I been around at that time. My heart fluttered, then sunk in a sea of star-crossed fate. *I mean, he's pretty hot, for the '80s.*

I fantasized, imagining what his whisper sounded like. What his lips tasted like. What his arm would have felt like around my shoulder, holding me close at the movies or strolling along the beach. *In the '80s we'd probably have been at a drive-in, and then what would have hap—*

"Atten-hut!" Mr. Womack snapped me back into the '90s. It was time to make our season debut.

Week after week, the band played on . . . but I would never be the same.

2004

"*Attention,*" the meditation teacher explained, "is one step from awareness of eternity."

It was my first meditation class, where one hour of seated practice was followed by a contemplative Q&A session. It happened to be in Hillsboro Beach, Florida, twenty miles due east of my old hometown of Coral Springs. A family crisis had drawn me back to Florida after two years of chasing the American Dream in Manhattan, New York, and Princeton, New Jersey, where my ex and I had attempted to build a life together. The daily regimen of playing a musical instrument had long been abandoned and now I needed some other way to reconnect with discipline and focus.

While I liked the idea of sitting still and practicing this mental yoga, unfortunately I had no idea what the teacher was talking about. So I raised my hand, and after a brief pause that felt like forever, he called on me.

"I don't understand the difference," I said before holding my breath.

"In attention, there is literally *a tension* between *what you perceive to be 'you'* and the object of focus," he said, pausing and patiently waiting for my exhale. "In awareness, or noticing, the sense that *you* are doing the focusing is absent—the appearance of tension dissolves and there is only awareness of What Is." He glanced into my eyes as if to ensure the words had penetrated.

But wait! Where had I seen those eyes before?

Spending the remainder of class trying to figure that out, I attained only a quivering state of non-transcendence.

I just couldn't remember.

∞

Four Nights Later

"Oh my *Gawd!*" I shouted.

My nerves were strung so high, my latent Long Island accent slipped out, revealing my roots as a native New Yorker posing as a laid-back Floridian. It was our first date and I did not like how this "meditation" teacher was driving my little Ford Probe—my precious worldly symbol of freedom that I was still very attached to.

He had offered to whisk me away with his own set of wheels, but I was too freaked out to brave his Honda Rebel, having once vowed to my mother that reading *Zen and the Art of Motorcycle Maintenance* was as close as I'd get to a hot-roddin' hog. I could not believe I'd accepted a date with the teacher I'd met just four nights ago.

Is it okay to date a guru?

"Relax," he said, gently patting my knee. My whole body melted and suddenly the girl who could hardly stop talking was rendered speechless.

I don't remember where we went that night—if we'd gone out to eat, to the movies, or to someplace else. I only remember this conversation we had while walking back to my bachelorette pad.

"I've seen you before," he said, "at Coral Springs High School."

Nice try, dude, I thought, *but pickup lines don't work on me anymore.*

"Ummm, but I already told you I went there so how can I believe you?" I inquired with five bats of my eyelashes, my inner romantic desperate to believe it was true.

"You were leaning over the water fountain outside the gym," he continued without flinching or looking down and to the right.

Questions flooded my brain. *Is he for real? Anyone could have taken a sip from that—*

"In 1992, I was there to coach at a wrestling tournament . . . "

Getting warmer, I mused, then challenged him with a question. To my delight, he nailed the name of our school's stud wrestler from that year.

He placed his arm around me. "You were wearing blue gym shorts and flipping your long brown hair out of your face, and out of the water fountain . . . "

Okay, yes. I had much longer hair at that time and he couldn't have known that from just seeing me now, I reasoned before doubt kicked in again. *But all of our shorts were blue, school colors.*

" . . . and you were holding a flute!"

I froze in my tracks. *Holy cow, I hadn't told him that. He was there!* There is just no way he could have known. I smiled as the jigsaw pieces of history started falling into place. Yes, the brunette leaning over the water fountain and sporting blue shorts could have been someone else, but the flute was the detail that wiggled him off the hook.

"You were radiant. I couldn't stop looking at you! I actually wanted to approach you then, however the age difference would have clearly been socially inappropriate."

As my jaw dropped to the floor, God placed a question on my tongue that I'd have never otherwise thought to ask. "Wait, did you play soccer for Coral Springs High in 1981?"

His lips turned a smile my soul instantly recognized. For one of the first times ever, I felt no need to fill up silence. I knew his eyes, his touch, his lips, his whisper. They were just as I had imagined. *Gulp!* My heart fluttered with the same butterflies as when I first saw his photo in the hallway.

As he leaned in, we touched foreheads . . . and then he answered, *"Now* do I have your attention?"

THE BOOK OF LOVE

*W*hen I realized that it was my teacher's 1981 All-State athlete portrait I'd stared at in my high school cafeteria back in 1992, twelve years before we met in person, I responded to his question, *"Now do I have your attention?"* with a simple *"Yes, you do."*

Two weeks later, those words became "I do." Though not in a court of law or a church, but by the sacred power of agreement.

And I started to write this book three months later.

With twelve weeks of marriage to my spiritual teacher under my belt, I was legit done people-pleasing to gain what I once considered to be love. I was sure I'd tasted the real thing now, which made me an expert, right?

I was going to write a book about it!

Yet when I finished drafting an Introduction, I didn't know how to begin Chapter One.

After years of pushing away any love that came my way, I stood on the verge of finally letting love into my life. But I still didn't know how to let down my defenses.

When I complained to him that no good chapter ideas were flowing, he said, "Maybe you're not ready to write a book about love because you don't know what it is yet."

"Fuck you! I know what love is!" I barked.

My response was the perfect evidence that he was right.

"You will write it one day. For now, just find out who's angry," he said without a flinch.

Although it did not feel like compassion at the time, it was the most loving thing he could have said. By guiding me to look for the one who was angry, I would no longer be able to project my anger onto him and ruin our relationship.

The patience arose within me to actually listen. I didn't want to wreck another marriage.

And that's the very first time I consciously witnessed my defenses dropping away.

Years of tension had led up to this moment. The year before we met, the divorce drama had siphoned most of my chi and I was out of strength to defend myself. I'd been on high alert ever since my first marriage began its final descent about midway through. Prior to this conversation about my "book of love," I never noticed my defenses were even there. *Was there some intangible entity standing guard, attempting to keep love out? Did it have teeth? Is that why I snapped? What was that thing?*

I became curious.

If it *was* a thing, maybe it wasn't evil, though. Maybe *it* was just trying to protect me from the type of hurt I'd experienced in the past when "love" appeared to be withdrawn by the husband whom it seemed I could never please.

Wait, was *this* the ego that spiritual authors talk about?

If viewed through a Kirlian photographic lens, this ego would have resembled a dark-red energetic vortex spiraling downward:

a tornado of internalized self-criticism. This wily whirlwind fueled what my parents and teachers praised as "perfectionism" and molded me into the academic achiever and homecoming queen people liked. It fed off the high-dosage cocktail of antidepressants and OCD meds coursing through my teenage veins. I quit these medications at nineteen upon discovering that they did not mix well with alcohol, but returned to them at twenty-seven, when the pain of divorce reached its zenith.

Years later, as I browsed the book archives in the office of the publishing company where I worked, my eyes were drawn to the "anger management" titles. So I scooped up armfuls of these and piled them on my self-prescribed reading stack. But a strange thing happened while I read those books. The concept of anger management seemed funnier by the minute, as I became aware of this inner heat called repressed anger.

How could anything this raw and explosive ever be controlled, let alone "managed"?

Despite the fact that I was back to popping antidepressants, and now tranquilizers to boot, the rage swelling up from my bowels could no longer be suppressed. I'd thought these drugs would keep it at bay . . . but they couldn't!

Because there was a problem.

In my year "between marriages," I'd started salsa dancing and having sex with a beautiful Puerto Rican man whose rhythmic motions, powerful hips, and dexterous hands proved the impossible: that as loaded up on chemicals as my body was, I was still a walking orgasm-waiting-to-happen. Despite the hellish anger and depression that arose the mornings after, the heavenly orgasmic releases I experienced in bed with him had catapulted me into a newfound awareness that life was pregnant with possibilities.

When I showed up at my Saturday therapy appointment eager to explore them all, my therapist didn't seem nearly as excited about my breakthrough. Instead, she insisted that I would require a series of at least six more sessions to rectify my "confusion." I respectfully asked how she came up with that number.

"You're *very* angry," she said.

I searched for the perfect reply as I stared past her unevenly mascaraed eyelashes into her eyes, but no words came. Instead, after I silently forgave myself for judging her makeup job, a deep wave of peace washed over me.

In the wake of this tranquility, the threat of anger lost its stronghold. I wasn't scared of my emotions anymore. The therapeutic methods she was using, which centered on verbally rehashing my personal history, no longer resonated with me. I only felt angry when dwelling on past grievances. Floating in an orgasmic state while dancing and making love had stopped my mind naturally, maybe for the first time. All I had to do was remember that joy, and I could viscerally feel the tension melting away. *So why "six" more of these sessions?* It didn't feel right in my heart to let her or anyone else have a say in how long the healing should take.

I finished that session respectfully but left her office curious about why she would not engage on the subject of orgasm with me. *What is she so afraid of? Perhaps she doesn't have experience in that area? Wait, this isn't about her, this is about me. Is she mirroring my resistance to sex, given the shame I've been carrying about my lustful desires and recent sexcapades? I think so.* She had likened shame and lust to repressed energies that got locked in the body because they were not allowed to be fully expressed. She'd provided me with Pulitzer Prize-worthy explanations of how the lovers I'd been drawing to me were vibrationally relative to my emotional scars: that men I'd deemed "assholes" were actually angels incognito, *helping me* to become conscious of the emotional baggage weighing me down. Now, *that* part of the therapy felt true—but once I became conscious of this weight on me, what was I to *do* with all this intel? Notify my girlfriends that I finally figured out why I keep attracting men who act just like my father?

What I *really* wanted to know was how I could transform repressed anger into a life of love and happiness. My creative writing teachers had exposed me to the notion that such transformation was possible through journaling, writing poetry, and other acts of pressing pen to paper. As much as I enjoyed writing, I couldn't express my mysterious instinct that sexual orgasm held a precious key to creating the same desired effect.

At the time, orgasm was the only experience that made me feel different, better, as if a true transformation was occurring without my having to "do" anything intellectual. Not that every orgasm I'd ever had felt transformative, because many times in the past orgasms even seemed to increase tension in my body, leaving me craving more sex only to release tension yet again. I'd also faked my share of orgasms so my lovers would feel that they'd satisfied me, to the point where I had felt disenchantment with sex. Intuitively, I sensed there had to be greater possibilities for orgasm than just a release of tension that left me with more residual tension. *But how would I ever experience these possibilities if I didn't let another man beyond my defensive barriers?*

Before I'd hit the dance floor and the sheets with my sultry Latino lover, I hadn't had an orgasm in over three years. And not for lack of trying!

I'd fallen for the idea that orgasm was impossible in a state of depression, especially because I'd started taking antidepressants again—which had paralyzed my libido and sensitivity. To this day, I know in my heart that it was grace that granted me access to the life-changing orgasms in my salsa days that opened my mind to a way out of depression and into heaven on earth.

Dropping me off after our first dinner date, my dance partner's parting words were: "Let's get together again before one of us gets cold feet." Believing at the time that the man should call me, I waited for the phone to ring and was disheartened when it never did. I moped around for days, muttering to myself that there was something irreversibly wrong with me.

This all went down one month before I met my teacher.

Words can't describe the ecstasy that emanated from my chest when we looked into each other's eyes for the first time. An emoji blend of Cupid's arrow and the pink growing heart could come close. That heart-bursting feeling lingered throughout our romantic courtship. It is still present today, though it has softened into something constant, subtle, and sublime. In the earliest days, my chest felt like an uncapped fire hydrant gushing with bliss. At the same time, my attention was *not* reaching outward toward him, like the old invisible claw that mentally groped past lovers, old dildos, and other objects of desire. Instead, my awareness remained centered, as if radiating from the center of my chest. Mystically, it felt as if this beautiful man were already inside of me.

Yet before I could write a book on the subject, I still had a lot to learn about love and how to let it in, never mind let it out. *How could I write about love . . .*

- *when I barely felt it for myself? Would I have to expose my secrets and let people see who I really was?*
- *when I felt guilty for desiring sex constantly?*
- *when I would have to let another man inside even though penetration felt physically painful?*
- *when I feared, even more, the pain of rejection?*
- *when I was so used to looking for love outside myself?*

Would I have to actually love myself first?

I hadn't a clue how any of this would happen. There was only one thing I could do: Be still and know *I Am*.

God surely possesses a sense of humor, with Nick being known by the name *I Am* when we met. As a spiritual teacher, he'd selected it not only because of its inherent truth, but also as a pedagogical tool, so when students called him by that name they would remember to sense and acknowledge their own being.

Well, it worked.

Don't Put a Face on Him

*W*hen I was seventeen, my secret wish for a sister finally came true. She was my first lesson in how the desires of our heart always come to us, though not necessarily on our schedule or in the precise way we imagine. Sometimes those skeletons in the family closet are alive and well! A kindred Irish-Italian, super-loving, water-sign brunette, Deb is my sister from my father's first marriage, though no sooner than I learned about her existence did he forbid us to see each other. It took me ten years to call her, but I when did we consummated our sisterhood over sushi and started hanging out often.

A few weeks prior to the night Nick and I met, Deb showed up at my apartment with a friend I didn't recognize. This voluptuous, earthy blonde looked stunning in her long green dress. Slung over her shoulder, an open tote revealed a Rider-Waite tarot deck and a crystal ball. Up to that point, anything new age had been taboo to me, but I conjured the courage to ask her if she would please do a reading on yours truly!

"Tarot cards or crystal ball?" she asked.

My pulse quickened. "Both, please."

"Okay then!" she smiled. "What life issue would you like to explore for insight?"

It was a no-brainer. Still, I blushed as I squeaked it out. "My romantic relationships."

First she laid ten cards out across my dining room table in a fancy arrangement and called it a Celtic Cross spread.

That sounds Irish and I'm part Irish, and it's a cross so it's gotta be okay. Please, God, and if not, forgive me. Amen.

As the woman flipped the cards one by one, she explained how they were like mirror reflections of my psyche, revealing clues to my own perceptions of my current challenges, past and future, hopes and fears, and other facets of my relationship life. A figure called the Hierophant appeared as she turned over the tenth card. This priestly male character sits on a throne between two Roman-style columns, a triple crown on his head and two golden keys at his feet.

"Turned upright, the Hierophant suggests to me that a powerful masculine teacher is present in your life, or about to be," she explained as she shuffled the deck. "The energy so strong, I'm being guided to do the whole spread again, if you agree."

Take two? Lucky me!

The tarot-inspired conversation turned out to be . . . *so fire.* Each time she turned a card over to reveal the image on its underbelly, she asked, "And what does this card symbolize to you?" before leaning in for my response. My mind lit up with insight. My words floated out like neatly folded paper airplanes that I could hear landing in her heart. I felt seen, I felt heard, and I was totally into it. And when we got to card ten again, she invited me to flip it. Yep, you guessed it . . . the Hierophant upright, again! She raised an eyebrow in Deb's direction. I suspected this was my big sis' ingenious way of spying on me for *la famiglia.*

"Double Hierophant upright in the tenth position, that's never happened," she said before packing up the deck. "The whole thing is auspicious in a way I can't explain, nor should I try to."

Is it good or bad that she can't explain it? Should I ask? Nah, just let it be.

"Can we still do the crystal ball?" I peeped.

At the time, I was dating two men who both had shaved heads and were well over six feet tall. One lived outside Atlanta, the other in Manhattan. I begged the clairvoyant in my living room to tell me if the man I was with in the crystal ball image had any hair. Expecting her to say no, implying that destiny would marry me with one of these two lovers, I about choked up my pepperoni pizza when she told me what I didn't want to hear.

"Yes," she said. Her brow was squinting in concentration, her tone serious. "Actually, he has *some* hair."

Some hair? WTF? I mean, it could have been either one of these men, caught during a phase when they'd let some of their hair grow in. I twisted her vision to suit my agenda. "Okay, is he tall?"

"Taller than you," she said.

Not helpful. I tried again. "Are we in a city?"

"You are on a mountain, and you are very happy together," she replied, then sighed and gazed up at me. "That is all I can see right now."

I waited a few weeks for either man to show up and whisk me away on a surprise mountain getaway, but it never happened. Eventually I moved on and met two other men. *(Gurarr!)* Both were taller and had "some hair." Then I realized that based on those criteria, my soul mate from the crystal ball *could have been almost any man out there!* I'd have to drop my image of what my dream man looked like.

This did not mean that I ceased my hunt for mountain men behind the wheels of vehicles with Wyoming, Montana, Arizona, New Mexico, Nevada, Colorado, Utah, California, Pennsylvania, and New York plates. Until at one particular red light at the corner of Hillsboro Boulevard and Powerline Road in Deerfield Beach, it hit me: I needed to keep my eyes on the road if I wanted to stick around to meet my future husband. Exhausted, I gave up the search right there.

And so ends the story of how I surrendered. In celebration, I pumped up my favorite tune, "As Long As You Love Me," on the car radio as the light turned green and the car rolled forward. I strained my vocal cords on the chorus, inadvertently repeating the affirmation that I didn't care who my lover was or where he was from. Man, I had no clue how prophetic my Backstreet Boys would turn out to be.

Names Are Vibrations, So I Chose Love

A year and a half after I stepped onto the spiritual path, I traced back through time, neatly printed the address of every house I'd ever lived in, and submitted the list to the Palm Beach County Clerk of the Court. Thanks to the judge's big red stamp, I was now officially known by the name I had chosen. It took me time to believe it myself. Because if you ever saw a photo of my parents, you'd know in a heartbeat that they were definitely not hippies who named me *Penelope Love*.

Those who knew me by my former name often asked me why I changed it. And when I didn't know them well enough to divulge the long story, I would say, "For the same reason Henry John Deutschendorf Jr. did."

"Who is that?"

"Only one of the most famous musicians in the world," I'd tease them before the big reveal. "John Denver."

To this day, I haven't met a person who doesn't agree that his stage name is more apropos. It's practically a jingle itself—poetic, musical, and memorable.

Yes, in fact, I too rationalized my name change in this way:

that having an unforgettable name would be essential to my work as a writer. But the real reason I changed it?

I could not resist.

Following the divorce in my late twenties, I felt torn about reclaiming the name my parents had assigned me at birth. I no longer felt like that person, nor did I wish to regress into the self-defeating behaviors I had associated with that name. Meditation had started to melt away my psycho-emotional baggage and the flame of insight was fueling my desire for freedom and rebirth.

About a year before my divorce, I'd read *Grace and Grit,* an intimate portrayal of contemporary philosopher Ken Wilber's writings spliced with diaries of his late wife, born Terry Killam. Her brilliant soul glorifies the name-change process as she explains why: "I changed my name to Treya." She said that she didn't get around to changing it for some time because, in her words, "I would have been embarrassed to change my name; my own judgment blocked me from 'following that dream.'" To this, I could so relate!

"How silly to change one's name!" she journaled. "What nonsense." But then Treya mused for two pages about how *she transformed when her name changed.* She began trusting herself and was kinder to herself. She closed her journal entry by celebrating her rebirth into a life "strengthened by my past but with a direction that is truly my own."[3]

Well, that hit me hard and I felt certain that one day I would change my name. *But to what?* I too was ready to be reborn, longing for a name to transfigure me from within by erupting the passion for life that had been smoldering inside for as long as I could remember. I searched for a name that by its very sound would arouse rapture within me. Something so lovely that maybe the sound of it would even evoke joy in others!

In the process, I reflected, "What's in a name?" Did it define me in any way? Especially in light of Shakespeare's "a rose by any other name would smell as sweet." *I felt the truth of that!*

However, I immediately discovered that my biological family did not quite share my enthusiasm.

But it didn't matter, because my life was never again to be about accommodating them. The politician within had died...yes, the people pleaser had left the building, forever!

In my earliest days of roaming the planet as Penelope Love, I worried that my coworkers thought I'd pushed the envelope of personal freedom too far. One of them started rumors that I was moonlighting as an exotic dancer (LOL, I wish I could dance so well). Still feeling defensive at the time, I concocted scientific reasons for my name change based on the research of Masaru Emoto, author of the *New York Times* Best Seller *The Hidden Messages in Water*.[4] (By the way, I highly recommend his books!)

Thanks to the docudrama *What the Bleep Do We Know?*, people around the globe were raving about Emoto's experiments. They revealed that water exposed to positive words formed beautiful, crystalline patterns of geometric complexity. In the face of negative words, the water crystals became deformed like toxic waste, if they took any shape at all. Thus, I rationalized, since the human body is nearly seventy percent water, and the brain is nearly ninety percent, my name change would affect the very composition of my body at the molecular level. This no doubt would affect the way I would feel. In attempting to convince others of this, I was convincing myself.

The significance of this choice could not be overestimated in my eyes, for it would function as *the* vibrational link to my self-expression among the known universe. Even before hitting Google, I knew Love would be my last name. To my inner word nerd, it was symbolic of "loving myself."

The forename decision proved more complicated. My carpal tunnel syndrome flared up as I *click, click, clicked* my way through the labyrinth of BehindTheName.com Given my penchant for textiles, knitting, and Greek mythology, I quickly found my attention captivated by my first and ultimate choice—Penelope!

Why? Because Penelope means "silent weaver," with the added benefit of a romantic origin fit for a Grecian queen. In Homer's *The Odyssey*, Penelope was the wife of Odysseus, king of Ithaca, who went off to battle in the Trojan War. While he was gone for twenty years, impatient suitors gathered to court her, unaware of her master plan to detain them. She wove a burial shroud for her father-in-law by day, and secretly unraveled part of it by night, in wait of her beloved to return. Meanwhile, word on the street was that only when the shroud was finished would she settle for another man.

I thought to myself, "Yes! This could be it."

By midnight, I'd finally narrowed my vast span of options to two: Penelope or Mariah.

Now here's where it gets mystical. The following evening was the one when I attended my first meditation class where Nick was then known by *I Am*.

In light of the prior evening's reconnaissance mission on the Internet, this totally fascinated me. So after class, I approached him and we kicked off our first intimate conversation with my nervous but brilliant pick-up line, "Could you tell me why you changed your name?"

I'll never forget his answer because it was completely unexpected, as he turned the question back on me. "What does it matter whether your name is Penelope or Maria, when you are always yourself?"

"Yes, that's true, I am always myself..." I exhaled, covered in full-body chills. *How the bleep did he know those were almost my exact choices?!*

Unless he were a world-class hacker who stayed up spying on strangers into the wee hours, there is simply *no earthly way* he could have decoded my dilemma: Penelope or Mariah? Yes, he'd left off the "h" in choice number two, but *c'mon!* I took it as a sign and in that instant, I became—

Penelope Love.

Somehow I felt as if the name had been chosen eons ago. As though it was already known by a much deeper part of myself than the frantic divorcée prowling the 'Net in search of a new identity.

Silently I stood in direct communion with that peaceful and all-knowing aspect of my being—that sensitive and loving presence radiating an intelligence beyond measure, such that it could have even funneled through the very mouth of my husband-to-be.

Two weeks later, Nick and I were married and the holy weaving of sexuality and meditation was underway. Up until then, knitting had been my closest portal to the meditative state. Never before could I set my needles down so fast! I blushed at God's sense of humor. Now that my name translated to silent weaver, and the Sanskrit word *tantra* meant "to weave," had I unwittingly fused my identity with sacred sex?

Following all my years of sexual suppression, the notion was thrilling and almost too much to take. But one thing was for sure: names were vibrations ... and I was now resonating with the frequency of love.

FOR THE LOVE OF MEN

*T*hroughout my childhood, the threat of being smacked with my father's belt gave me all the incentive I needed to behave my little self. My choices—about what to do, who to play with, what to wear, and eventually who to date—boiled down to whichever option would rattle my father least. Though my mother was generally accepting of my life, my father let his disapproval be known via explosive verbal assaults. It didn't matter what I chose. In his eyes, unless he made a decision for me, it was wrong. For much of my life thereafter, it was not the approval of women I was seeking, but that of men. And not only a few men, most of them.

My compulsive seeking of men's approval knotted me up inside. On the surface, it appeared I was very much approved of, as much as anyone could possibly need to be. I earned straight-A report cards and academic honors bestowed by my school's male principal. In athletics, I butterflied and breaststroked my heart out to win races, but more importantly to impress my coaches—yep, men. I flourished in middle and high school musical contests under the guidance of male band directors. I launched a community literacy program with the enthusiastic support of a male administrator. And the crowning moment? Being pronounced homecoming queen on the field before all of the football players who were otherwise unaware of my nerdly existence.

In order to generate spending money for clothes to attract men at college, I worked on a team of mostly male grocery baggers. I earned a scholarship named after the man who owned that grocery chain. I married a man right out of college, stepped into a coveted media position with a prestigious foundation under an all-male hierarchy in my department, and then climbed the corporate ladder to chief magazine editor for a well-known publisher, where my need for approval magnetized—you guessed it—more male bosses! As each of these men celebrated various successes with me, could I have simply enjoyed the moment? Nope. Not for an instant. I was too busy analyzing every crease of their smiles and the degree of rapture in their eyes for some confirmation that they might have fallen hopelessly in love with me forever. In my depths, however, no stamp of approval ever left me feeling adored by any man for more than a fleeting moment.

I'd read enough self-help books to understand that I had to love myself first before I'd ever feel the reciprocated love of another. These authors made it sound so simple, but I didn't know how to love myself. Still, at the time, arrogance prevented me from admitting this. *I already love myself,* I thought. And so over the course of three decades, my life came to resemble that of the costume jewelry I'd picked over on boutique sale racks: it looked almost pretty, but it was not worth buying because it lacked that dazzling, beautiful quality that made me want to own it. I'd gone silently insane, not only from shopping to enhance my appearance for men's viewing pleasure, but from scrutinizing their faces for signs that I was a stone-cold knockout!

With each sign, I grew more addicted. The more approval I got, the more I wanted; the more I wanted, the more I got. It was a lusty loop that lasted until the fifth and final year of my first marriage. Once my husband started paying more attention to his entrepreneurship than our relationship, the withdrawal symptoms set in. Constant trembling manifested as the body's effort to shake off deep-rooted anxiety. When it didn't stop, I called my mother crying. And my therapist? She was on speed-dial. I was a certifiable train wreck. Because of the impossible expectations I placed on men to desire me, I resented those from whom I wanted love but was denied it. Yet if I 'fessed up to all this neurotic baggage, what man would ever love me then?

I worried about this as I roamed the beach during an addiction research work conference in San Juan, Puerto Rico, in June 2004. On that scalding summer day, the question haunted me: *Will I ever find true love?*

Unbeknownst to me, I'd soon fly home and meet *The One* at meditation. And days later, we'd be cuddling and discussing the mysteries of the universe on an oceanfront balcony under the stars. I was feeling him out to see if he believed true love was possible. In place of a simple yes or no, he unleashed this bomb on me:

"Do you believe God is infinite?"

"Yes," I said.

"And doesn't infinity leave room for all things?"

Yes!

Blissful in his arms, I couldn't fall asleep. *Did I just forfeit all of my excuses—forever?* I contemplated this until the dawn of its stunning conclusion: within infinity, there would always be a *yes* where I truly wanted one to be.

Dear God!

There is no going back to sleep.

PART TWO

Love Is Not
What You Think

One Last Lap

My therapist implored me,
"Bring him down to earth."

Her commandment catalyzed
a surge of true self-worth.

Codependent?
No more
nor would I dream
that way
again.

He was not a man
bound by laws of this realm.
In his eyes I spied
infinity at the helm.

Even as I cried
this therapist denied
my heart open wide.

There was no going back,
it was already done;
I saw him as The One
with whom I'd fly
into the sun!

Of course I love this place:
each moment I say grace
for the chance to run
one last lap
of the human race.

Yet in these bones I'd felt
to summon him
back to earth
would defy
the sole and
sacred purpose
of our birth.

DISOWNED

*S*ince the day I met Nick, meditation on the infinite I, or what is always here, became the cornerstone of my spiritual practice. I found that contemplating this had the same effect as love, instantly lifting me to the heaven I was taught awaited me after death. All contradictions were resolved, not by watching my breath but by turning inward and merging with the awareness aware of my breath. *How invigorating!*

I was in love and finally at peace.

However when I shared this exhilaration with my parents, the humans I thought would be happiest for me, I detected not one iota of excitement. During what turned out to be my last visit to their house, I'd entered through the garage into the kitchen, where both my mother and my father were sitting at the newspaper-covered table, drinking coffee, and watching cable news. After walking over and giving them each a kiss, I scooped up Carlee, the Bichon, who had been scratching up my freshly shaven legs since I tiptoed in.

"What's new?" my father asked between puffs of his cigarette, his eyes never leaving the TV set.

"Well, I went to meditation," I managed to eke out between dog kisses to my chin. "And I love it because I just know it's going to help heal my OCD."

My mother bent down to wipe up the pee-pee puddle at my feet. "It would be good, if it does that, right hon?" she said, looking up at him.

My father stood up, turned his back to us, and grabbed a can of soda from the fridge. "OCD or no OCD, it better not be a fuckin' cult!" With that, he stormed out, the shuffle of his slippers echoing like match strikes, ratcheting up the fire of his rage.

When I was growing up, this same man had been a good provider who was always there for me, though not in a spiritual sense or even in the Hallmark way. Rather, he could be found in the frame of the garage door watching me coming and going, scrutinizing the length of my skirts, counting my bites of dessert, tallying my babysitting income, and picking up the landline receiver to track my every second of phone time, it seemed. I came to appreciate him as an antagonist in my life story, but not before the dozens of times he reminded me how I'd disgraced our family. Which I'd never comprehended because how could a few moments of kissing my high school boyfriend in our driveway strip away the lifetime of being his pride and joy?

"But the neighbors, they saw you and now they think your mother and I raised a tramp!" he said.

That particular memory floated like raw sewage on the surface of my mind. Within a few months, my deepening meditation practice broke the dam and a flood of early-life memories came rushing back in HD with surround sound. I remembered my father's voice from my earliest days of life, like the sharp edge of a samurai sword, slicing through the air and sending my teeny body into trembling fits. Eventually I recalled the cigarette smell, his grunting, raspy breath, and the sheer size of his naked body in orange underwear, approaching me on the edge of my parents' bed before everything went black. And despite the horror of this recollection, something in my soul still loved the reminiscence of his kinder forms of touch and the resonance of his Brooklyn parlance. In over a decade of therapy, I had tried desperately to reconcile these mixed emotions and fathom his fiery temper, irrational views, and contradictory behaviors, to no avail; yet, through meditation, I found acceptance and compassion for the sorrows and pain underlying his constant yelling. But I never succeeded at unraveling the mystery of how I, as much as I loved him and in spite of it all, became a target of one of his vendettas.

Everyone who knew my family had an opinion about this first-generation Italian-American telephone man who spent hard-working days in relative isolation weaving wires and scaling poles that, ironically, helped people communicate. Most people who wanted to get to know my mother, brother or me had to "go through him first" and so they perceived us in his shadow. My mother was revered as a saint for remaining quiet and composed, even as he wielded his verbal abuse at servers, cashiers and other innocent bystanders minding their own business. My brother was saluted for national athletic success in youth swimming despite our father's eye on his every flip-turn and the screaming critiques on the drive home from practice. I, on the other hand, received the highest praise for remaining loyal to him, despite how his screaming at the three of us mortified me in front of my friends, who had long lost interest in coming over.

For my submissive "good behavior," I was admired by family near and far—until D-Day.

The day my father disowned me was like any other day, really, only better. It had finally happened: the shameful event, the curse I feared worst, the thing I'd walked on eggshells my entire life to avoid was now at hand. Having summoned the courage to stand up to his attacks, I would survive to tell the tale, to breathe the air, to taste Freedom—a whole new F-word for me! But for a girl who had spent a majority of her Saturday nights as a teenager snuggled up with *The Bell Jar** by Sylvia Plath, freedom was an acquired taste. My father had been battling my attempt at an adult-to-adult conversation. Over the phone, I was telling him I did not want to invest in the Boca Raton condo that he had chosen for me in cahoots with a real estate agent. I'd never heard of her, but she had called me earlier that day, on my father's orders, to discuss the property.

"Live there," he ordered. "Meet and marry a doctor, instead of that asshole Nick, I Am, David Koresh or whatever his fucking name is . . ."

"No, Dad," I said. "No!"

I heard him take a drag on his cigarette. I could practically smell the stench of the wheezing that preceded his final blow: "You're not my daughter anymore! You ungrateful bitch! You . . . you're dead to me!"

As those words rang through the receiver, I did not find myself living out a dreadful episode of the *Sopranos* or *Shark Tank*.

I simply . . . sat there . . . being . . . letting it sink in.

In those few words, he'd stripped me of my daughter identity, the I.D. card that had caused me more grief, shame, and pain than all my other false identities combined. It was like a noose of fear that had been suffocating me all my life snapped. It stung fiercely, but then suddenly . . . relief!

In an instant, as if to soothe my broken heart, *it* enveloped me: the inexpressible grace. I was overcome by the love and support of the infinite, indivisible God.

So light was this freedom from tyranny! Yet it wasn't long before I began to fret: *If my own father didn't want me, what man ever would? Could the man my father disowned me over love me without conditions? Would marrying this man be worth the risk of losing the*

---

* A 1963 American novel about a suicidal woman's descent into mental illness.

"love" of my earthly father, however dysfunctional it had been? Because until then, conditional love was the only kind of love that had seemed real to me.

Why did my flesh-and-blood father disown me? Was there a reason besides his stated hatred for Nick, although they never met? Was it because Nick had encouraged me to stand up to my father? Was he reacting to the fact that I could no longer be controlled? Was he afraid that he no longer had a say in my life choices?

Who wants to know?

Ironically in all my years of Sunday school, I'd never heard the parable of the hundred sheep, until Nick referenced his King James Bible in *satsang* that week:

> "How think ye, if a man have an hundred sheep, and one
> of them be gone astray, doth he not leave the ninety and
> nine, and goeth into the mountains, and seeketh that which
> is gone astray?" (Matthew 18:12)

Now I was the one sheep, and all I could do was pray God would be in search of me. If a daughter disowned is not her father's daughter anymore, what is she?

What transpired emotionally over the next decade would pave the pathway to forgiveness. I came to honor my complex relationship with this man who, despite his monstrous actions, carried me home from the hospital, saw that I was fed daily, warmed our home by paying the bills, contributed financially to my academic and extracurricular activities K through 12. Understanding these as privileges,

I thanked him over and over but no amount of gratitude was ever enough. Evidently he was just not capable of receiving it. Perhaps guilt over his history of sexually abusing me had blocked his heart.

I also looked carefully at the word "disowned" and what it implied, and took responsibility for my role in the tango. In my true essence as awareness, I had never been a victim, nor had I been owned by my father. Yet, I too had claimed my father as my own. In pure spirit, he was not mine any more than I was his. This had to happen. For both of us.

No longer was I indebted to him or anyone.

Disowned. No longer owned. No longer welcome in my parents' home. It didn't make sense at the moment, but in time I understood the prosperity lesson in this, too. I'd been given a gift money can't buy. My life! No longer able to depend on my father or mother for money, I was guided to God's inexhaustible supply. Only then did I become a student of lessons in true faith, one of which was that my biological father was not my supply: God was. All along it had been God providing through him; the man called my father was not my provider. Perhaps the human belief that he had been my provider had let him feel entitled to order me around. Maybe it was designed this way—to build the pressure that snapped our cord of attachment. Any relationship would have to snap under the weight of such immeasurable expectations.

What amazes me now is how dependent relationships have their own self-destruct mechanism built right into them. In this case, all the cursing and the disowning turned out to be divine grace at work. It literally forced transcendence of all inherited identities: the little girl, the feeble child incapable of surviving in the world without her parents, the woman who could not exist without a man financing her existence.

My God, isn't that too much pressure to put on *anybody*?

I doubt there's a single soul who enjoys being disowned and called ungrateful. Yet, in the end, I am grateful it happened, because it taught me about the nature of conditional love and planted the seeds of contrast in my heart, so that true love could blossom and flourish. It led me to the Eden of freedom, a space from which it's possible to say "I love you, Dad," and mean it. Except that, he never heard it. He couldn't hear it. He couldn't hear it because he wanted control, he wanted to be right.

No more.

HURRICANE I AM

*M*y mother had always referred to it as "living in sin," when a couple shared a home prior to tying the proverbial knot. I had managed to steer clear of it with my first husband, who didn't cosign a lease with me until after our trip to the altar. In hindsight, I don't believe that cohabitating before marriage would have changed our fate. When we separated and I rented my own apartment, residing with a new lover was the furthest thing from my mind. So liberating it was, living solo and decking out my bachelorette crib according to my girly whims. I wanted to enjoy coming home to my own space, one that felt like an authentic expression of my divine feminine soul.

The first time it hit me that I'd no longer have to consider anyone else's decorating tastes, I was in Sam's Club at around 8:45 p.m. following a tiresome day at the office. I had gotten sucked in to the labyrinth of the wholesale fortress built out of super-duper cereal boxes, king-size rice sacks, monolithic muffins, and titanic toilet paper rolls lying in wait. My cart was brimming with twenty-first century nesting essentials: printer ink, oversized bath towels, an electric piano keyboard, frozen veggie medleys, microwavable burritos, defrostable mini quiches, a new blender, a portable foot spa, and a year's supply of razor cartridges to keep my legs silky smooth for the next man who would walk down these aisles beside me. For the time being, however, no one on earth knew where I was. Not a husband, not parents, not a friend; no one had a trace on me. Not even the CIA! At least it felt that way. If I wanted to be out shopping this late, no one could tell me what to do or otherwise interrogate me when I walked in the door. While I diddled in the self-checkout line, the thought flashed through me like a bolt of lightning: *So this is what it feels like to be free!*

The body-numbing fluorescent lights inside the market faded behind me as I rolled my stuffed cart into the darkness of the deserted parking lot. I became addicted to this rush. Not only this impostor bliss but the excitement of bringing it all home and organizing my precious purchases into their perfect little place in my killer babe abode! My unique genetically coded variation of the nesting instinct was in full force. I routinely raced from Starbucks to work to the stores to home, Monday through Friday, 8:30 a.m. to 10:00 p.m.; Saturday and Sunday were for returns of items that did not make the cut in my one-bedroom, one-bathroom shakti pad. Georgia O'Keeffe reprints covered the bedroom walls, as testament to my extreme femininity. Each night, as I lifted my purple duvet, slipped between the layers of one-thousand-thread-count Egyptian cotton sheets from Bed, Bath and Beyond, I prayed for someone to share all of this with me. It was actually not a problem finding men who were willing to enjoy the silky white sheets, as an epidemic of one-night stands led me into deeper states of panic that could only be cured by ... yep, more shopping!

I nested, and I nested, and I never rested. The reality of that hit me one night when my sister visited. On the sofa, her feet kicked up on the coffee table, Deb surveyed the masterpiece I had created with approval in her eyes but a query that didn't match: "Do you ever just sit down, right here, like this?" Like a condor's wings, her arms spread wide then flopped to her sides, shamelessly creasing my throw pillows.

As I stood there staring at her, my annoyance with her cute leather pumps on my furniture melted away when her arrow of a question pierced the bullseye of my overcaffeinated ego. I was certain she was a tad envious of the catalog style and cleanliness of my apartment, and I'm not sure it was meant as an intervention, but her inquiry had that effect. And before I joined her on the couch, rum and Diet Cokes in the Crate and Barrel serving tray in my hands, I answered her with the honest truth. "No," I said, "but I'd really like to."

"Well, siddown, Sis," she said. "Let's drink to that!"

"Cheers!" I said over the clink of our Pottery Barn tumblers, making a mental note that *this* was precisely what my therapist had been talking about—that sometimes I needed to sit down and just do nothing.

Aha! This was why my therapist was prescribing meditation.

The sixty-day notice for my lease renewal arrived the morning after I first attended meditation, and for some reason I hesitated to sign it. Which meant it sat on the kitchen counter during those two weeks between the night I met Nick and the day we decided to marry each other in that very apartment. Although I'd had a month to decide whether to stay or give notice, I felt clear in my heart that I wanted to move in to the ashram and devote myself to my new spiritual practice.

Yet as Nick pointed out when he slept over, there was no way I could bring all of my stuff with me. Not only was there not enough physical space, but the spiritual path was about releasing attachment to personal possessions that had nothing to do with happiness. The simple truth burned ... like a torch! It lit my heart on fire and I felt ready—oh so ready!—to let go and surrender to God's will, releasing anything holding me back from true happiness.

That's when I took a deep breath and surveyed the 360-degree scene of books, furniture, wall art, and perfectly placed potpourri dishes until all the air in my lungs finished pushing through my pursed lips. I had no idea what to toss first. *Not the fish tank where my twin-flame goldfish, Simon and Simone, live, oh not the VCR— do you know how many movies I almost watched with that?—and definitely not the plastic lemon tree ... can he not see how flawlessly it's lending feng shui to the foyer?!* Still, I played it cool.

"I can't do it, but I will let you," I said to Nick as I jiggled the key ring to my IKEA princess castle and tucked it into his palm. It was 8:15 a.m. and magazine proofs were waiting for me on my desk. Following a quick-ish kiss on the lips, I dashed off to work. On my way, I called the leasing office and left a message that I'd be moving out in five days. *Yikes!*

When I arrived home that evening, the door was locked so I knocked, figuring Nick was inside. Just then he ravished me from behind with a bear hug and kisses and said with a twinge of Wisconsin accent, "Perfect timing! I just finished the last trip to the dumpster."

"To the dumpster?" I said, not remembering in that moment what I'd given him permission to do.

"Ready to go in?" he said, looking in my eyes as he unlocked the deadbolt.

Click. Click.

I stepped in and there it was. My apartment looking very much like the day I moved in—walls completely bare, floor-to-ceiling empty space, with only a naked couch and table in the center of the living room.

If this is what's left out here, then how much is left in the bedroom? I wondered, feeling jolted yet oddly calm under the circumstances. There was, literally, almost *nothing* to be upset about.

As I tiptoed into the bedroom, I gasped with relief that he had, as we agreed, filled several boxes with my CDs, computer equipment, and clothing. I knew I could trust him and he had come through! I jumped into his arms and kissed him with childlike thrill.

"Anything left in the bathroom?" I asked.

"Take a look," he said, waving me in. It was shower-curtain and rug-free, and save the half-used roll of toilet paper, there was no evidence of human life within it. I took a deep breath and caught a whiff of Lysol. He had even cleaned! *Well,* I thought, *I am ready to live in the ashram.*

"Would you like to take a walk to the dumpster and see the aftermath?" he asked.

"Sure!" I chimed, laughing at his innuendo to "Hurricane I Am," the tongue-in-cheek term we had given this operation of cleansing out my abode in preparation for the big move in. It was July 2004 and Florida was climbing toward the height of hurricane season. Thinking of it as a hurricane helped because after a hurricane blew through, if I was fortunate enough to survive, I'd still have what was really important: my life.

If I want freedom and I have to let go of all my things to make that happen easier, so be it, I reassured myself. Then I said, "Let's go!"

We strolled, with arms around each other to the trash area of the parking lot. As you can imagine, when I set foot inside the concrete-walled area surrounding the dumpster, my heart leapt up into my throat, tears choked my eyes, and I yelped.

Just for a moment, I wanted to dive into the wreckage and salvage it all: the floral scrap books and photos scattered about everywhere, my high school yearbook, old love letters, nail polishes, lipsticks, CD cases, my college textbooks, and graduate school diploma—already splattered with other visitors' empty French-fry containers, cigarette butts, and God knows what else. Further down, beneath someone's wet, split-open garbage bag, I spied my purple bed sheets and moaned a massive *"Uggghhh!"* The colorful, and now crumpled, Georgia O'Keeffe reprints were the hardest to face. Then, I took one last glance at my cluttered history, covered my eyes . . . and no more.

I cried, and I cried, and I cried the whole walk back to the place I once called home. Nick let it all be—the grunting, the snot dripping, the choking in disbelief. Had my matrix just been deleted? He didn't comfort me and somehow that comforted me. And suddenly, the waterworks shut off, I looked him in the eye, we stood at the door of the apartment and I said, "Let's go home."

As we drove north on the turnpike, I never felt lighter or more free in my entire life. With the removal of so many things that pulled my attention outward, I was now able to turn inward. *So this is what it feels like to be free!*

I laughed and I cried tears of indescribable joy. Nick and I were not married in the eyes of any church but I knew moving into the ashram would be the furthest thing in the universe from "living in sin." In fact, it would be living with purity and peace, with acceptance of whatever happens as the will of God. It would mean embracing a new type of family who supported me with putting God first, one in which all my kin continually pointed me back to remembrance of my true Self. The perpetual presence of love within its walls would be a daily reminder of the revelations of Hurricane I Am:

I am not my things and I can weather any storm.

MEDICATION TO MEDITATION

*O*f all the falling dominoes that led me to the ashram, the first was my therapist. Six months before I attended *satsang*, her efforts to teach me a basic meditation technique began enticing me off her couch and onto the zafu cushion.

"Now that your body has adjusted to the antidepressants, tell me . . . how are your meditations coming along?" she inquired, peering over her leopard-print reading glasses.

I didn't like it when she stared at me this way.

"Okay," I replied, evading eye contact by fixating on her towering mound of blond hair.

The dismal truth? I had tried to meditate for one agonizing minute that morning before throwing my hands up. Yet the photograph of the actress Heather Graham meditating on the cover of *TIME* remained emblazoned in my mind. *I want to be peaceful and radiant like that.* The magazine no one seemed to be reading at my parents' house had found an honorary place on my coffee table. After poring over the overwhelming research about "how meditation can train the mind and reshape the brain,"[5] I felt determined to continue trying. My unresolved emotions about the Big D, as I was calling my divorce, were buried under layers of workaholism, antidepressants, and a covert love affair with lattes, chocolate chip scones, and everything sweet. I'd numbed myself to where I couldn't muster a single tear over the shambles of my freshly failed marriage. Still, I was willing to do just about anything to feel better—yep, even if it meant "the impossible": sitting for five minutes every day without moving.

At my last therapy session, I'd stated my intention to practice. Yet rather than actually relaxing, I dedicated the time to "figuring out" how to meditate correctly, which launched a new pattern that lasted eight months. This entailed spending high percentages of my paychecks on candles, crystals, CDs, and other "enlightenment gear," beating myself up when the bill came, and then licking my wounds, along with pints of Häagen-Dazs Dulce de Leche. All this to tightly pack down frequent outbursts of rage over my inability to find the mind's off switch. What I was doing was anything but meditating. The more that Thich Nhat Hanh's recording nagged at me, "Witness your thoughts," the more I fantasized about getting up off my zafu and throwing it at the CD player!

After scratching "watch my breath" off my to-do list, I asked my therapist to tell me more about that thingy called a "mantra."

"I'm a writer, a word person, so I think that a mantra will definitely help me," I said. Okay, so I successfully justified my way out of silence, once again.

In a valiant attempt to teach me Transcendental Meditation, a.k.a. TM, she guided me to choose one word to focus on.

"That's easy," I said. "Love."

"Love it is," she affirmed as she jotted it in her notebook. "When you get home from work, sit for five minutes in your favorite chair, close your eyes, breathe deeply and focus on the word *love*."

"Can I pet my kitten while I do it?"

"No."

Kitty or no kitty, it didn't work.

As I stroked my Calico's fur, I launched a prayer into the universe for formal meditation instruction from an experienced teacher in a class-style format.

Enter, the twenty-four-year-old Adonis who referred me to the ashram just one week later.

"What's it like to really meditate?" I probed him to tell me during our second sex date.

"I can't explain it, you just have to go and experience it with I Am or a teacher like him," he said. "And it's not your typical style of meditation, it's called Self-inquiry." As you'll recall, this sentiment was echoed on our break-up call two days later.

At least he'd had the courtesy to convey his intentions, rather than secretly date other women while my claws became more deeply embedded in his hunky bod. Rejected as I'd felt in that moment, I also felt strangely respected in a way—one that seemed to tie back together the loose threads of my self-esteem, at least to where I felt worthy of drying off my tears and trying this Self-inquiry thing. I later found out it was Nick who'd advised this young man to call and communicate his truth. This indirectly led me to consciously choose between an open relationship and monogamy.

I wanted monogamy, but more than that, I wanted to learn meditation.

When I attended class the following week, my first question for Nick during the Q&A portion was about the difference between meditation and Self-inquiry. "Meditation is fixing attention on one idea to the exclusion of all others," he explained, "while Self-inquiry is fixing your attention on your Self, making your Self that one idea."

While contemplating this, my eyes kept being drawn to the portrait of a white-bearded man with kind eyes, hanging on the wall behind Nick. When I raised my hand again to ask who it was, Nick said, "Ramana Maharshi." He then told the story of Ramana's awakening as a sixteen-year-old boy when an intense fear of death drove his mind inward, and how he became aware of "the voice of the 'I' within"[6] that endured regardless of what was happening with his body. From this space of inner awareness, several questions arose in him including, *"Is the body 'I'?"* [7]

When I got home that evening, my inner investigative journalist made a beeline for the computer. *Who was this man that so poignantly questioned the I-thought?* According to Google, he was an Indian sage who had lived between 1879 and 1950. His teaching was a no-frills approach to Self-inquiry, both praised and criticized for its simplicity. Across various websites, I spied the same photograph of him looking like a wise grandfather. Being that YouTube wasn't a thing at the time, I couldn't access a video to check him out, so Amazon's "Look Inside the Book" was all I had to go on. To my surprise, the Foreword of *The Spiritual Teachings of Ramana Maharshi* [8] was an essay by Carl Jung, who wrote of him, "In India he is the whitest spot in a white space." [9] I was still a little scared of the Eastern-ness of Maharshi's ideas, but I reasoned that if he was good enough for the spiritual godfather of psychoanalysis, this book just might improve my life somehow. I one-click ordered it, intrigued that Jung's essay framed his life and teachings as a "message to a humanity which threatens to lose itself in the chaos of its unconsciousness and lack of self-control."[10] Maybe this Self-inquiry thing could help me rise above the unconscious patterns of addictive behavior once and for all!

Nick made Self-inquiry relatable, introducing it through a contemplative form of yoga called *jnana*, the path of enlightenment through wisdom and insight. I enjoyed practicing it in satsang and contemplating the teaching on my own. This was a high-level yoga that demanded nothing of my muscles and joints, yet it somehow helped me to become more flexible in every way.

And because it was not done in front of a mirror, it released the habit of identifying with my body's reflection as myself. I could practice it anywhere: on the couch, in bed, in the shower, in the car, in line at the grocery story, and even at work!

Through the clear lens of *jnana*, I saw through the mechanism of depression and addiction, both of which reinforced the schizophrenia of a separate sense of "me." To my astonishment, it revealed that addiction to thinking was the primary addiction. Even the thought "I'm so depressed, I need (something) to lift me up" is only a thought itself.

Coffee often, albeit temporarily, filled that hole—and it was not the best part of waking up, wrapping my brain around the fact that the desire for coffee was just an emotion-linked thought floating around my psyche. Especially because the body that I called "I" experienced a barrage of related thoughts (e.g., craving, thirst, caffeine-withdrawal headaches, etc.) that felt visceral and "real" whenever I went without my cuppa. Yet, this new *jnana* yoga had given me something else to "do" instead of complain—it had me watching my thoughts like a cat on a mouse hole. Every *thing* was just a thought, and every *thought* was just a thing. And that made coffee a thought I was aware of—and when I simply stayed aware of it, not consuming it or otherwise being consumed by thoughts about it, there was peace!

I accepted my caffeine addiction and all of my thoughts, because what else could I do? Such is the nature of mind: *it thinks.* In this case, the practice of *jnana* had slowed down my racing mind to a snail's crawl, whereby I could notice the peace. Out of that stillness arose the *aha!* I could pinpoint three separate thoughts related to the story *I am / addicted / to coffee:* (1) the illusion of myself as a body starring as "I," (2) the craving or attachment itself, and (3) the coffee. How simple, right? These three thoughts had been looping back in on one another, preventing me from seeing the "I-thought" stringing them all together. I was aware of them all! Without *jnana*, how else could someone ever see it?

Another exquisite revelation then followed. I asked myself, *precisely what happened when I drank a cup of coffee?* Well . . . I stopped wanting coffee and the mind became still, albeit very briefly. Why? Because the craving-thought had been temporarily replaced with the "I-am-satisfied" thought—and no doubt some serotonin. Yet, since my conditioning was that "I need my coffee to wake up" and "I enjoy the caffeine rush," the desire for my cup of joe just kept circling back again. Mistakenly, I was attributing the bliss of a still mind to the coffee *rather than to the cessation of thoughts* that *always* follows the fulfillment of *every* desire.

Jnana and Self-inquiry worked! And not only to help me get "off the coff" . . . I shed a bunch of other crutches too. Because now it was my own direct experience: whenever I felt the body as "I" or "me," suffering loomed in the wings, because the course of suffering happens to a body. And when I somehow detached from this false identification that I am "only a body," I was liberated from bondage and life became a heaven.

So after masquerading for all those years as a compulsive engine, the mind was only a small part of "I," from which I breathed life. I finally felt the truth of Einstein's quote: "No problem can be solved from the same level of consciousness that created it."[11] In other words, *the mind cannot solve the problems of the mind.* Eureka! I saw the pleasure-pain drama of addiction at its core, as just an endless cycle of thoughts, like cannibals feeding off themselves without mercy. The key to recovery was therefore not in the thoughts themselves, but rather in finding out *who* or *what* is thinking the thoughts—and then *fixing my attention on the awareness itself.*

Nick often referred to Self-inquiry by its Sanskrit name, *atma-vichara*, describing it as "a meditation on the meditator." I fell in love with this paradoxical practice of turning inward to meditate on myself as "I." It raised questions that had no verbal answer. To a word-person like me, this startled my entire being until the shock morphed into great relief. The underlying silence that pervades everything lured me to the edge of surrender: releasing all thoughts, all questions, and all answers to the inner questioning, "Who is thinking?"

I cannot emphasize enough how valuable this inquiry proved to be. The pursuit "Who am I?" turned out to be the off switch to the mind's flood of thoughts and compulsions. (And also very important was, when a thought arose, I learned to not resist it or try to replace it with yet a better one, which only sustains thinking.)

Whatever the thought was, I investigated, *"Who is thinking this thought?"* and the obvious response was always, "I am." When I then affirmed myself by *feeling* "I am," I became acutely aware of the felt-sense of "I." Remaining aware of this feeling of "I," before any other thoughts could arise, I'd look in vain, *"Who am I?"* *Voilà!* The Holy Grail. With the question "Who am I?" (or sometimes I asked, *"What am I?"*), the mind was withdrawn back into its Source. Then, right there, in the gap between successive thoughts, there was and ever is only pure awareness, transcending all experience. This, and this alone, is pure Being. The truth had dawned—*the deeper this sense of Being becomes, the more peaceful I become.* And when I then become conscious of anyone or anything, there is love.

Many have heard the parlance chiseled into the Temple of Apollo at Delphi: "Know Thyself." Well, this is It! This is that Knowing of Self, Self-awareness.

Eventually I came to understand exactly why Adonis insisted, "I can't explain it, you just have to go and experience it." I would later learn that proper Self-inquiry instruction transcends all descriptions because it involves experiential dimensions most often conveyed within the context of a lineage, living teacher to student. As a writer I have tried to do it justice but it is impossible to convey the teaching in writing alone, for the written word—much like a dead guru—does not kick ass! Picture the existential detectives in *I Heart Huckabees* played by Lily Tomlin and Dustin Hoffman, furtively peering through the bathroom window at Jason Schwartzman's character, Albert Markovski, brushing his teeth, jotting down notes on his every move. Much like Albert, I had signed up for it, metaphorically speaking, by asking Nick and the other ashram residents to similarly point out my areas of unconsciousness. Through receiving such unrelenting guidance, I learned to effectively utilize the mind's compulsive tendencies as an effective trigger, harnessing and focusing mental energy that had long fueled destructive habits, to powerfully *redirect* the mind back to the Source of pure, unconditioned Consciousness—prior to thinking. Most people are almost completely unaware of this aspect of their Being.

Before I'd discovered Self-inquiry, it felt impossible to rest for extended periods in the peacefulness of the no-mind state. Although witnessing my breath and my thoughts directed my mind into a one-pointed focus, it did not ultimately succeed in retaining the mind in its source because separation always remained in my awareness: that is, a sense of distance between me *and* the breath being meditated on or thought being noticed. *This* is the perception of separation that sustains duality—it now made sense why peace had seemed impossible to me. Self-inquiry, on the other hand, stills or absorbs the mind completely. With each absorption into pure stillness, the mind further loses its grip of attachments, so compulsive thoughts and addictive conditioning fade away. Self-inquiry withdraws mind-made seductions into the timeless realm, the peaceful state one may aim for countless times and yet still fail to attain without this wisdom.

After repeatedly abiding in sustained periods of Self-aware-ness through *jnana* and Self-inquiry, I came to know existence as a tangible sense of love, so deep and utterly consuming that herein self-destructive thoughts and tendencies neither emerge nor manifest into physicality. As such, Self-inquiry has become my go-to panacea for all ailments. *Who* would have imagined it could be so simple?

Indeed "I" would have.

Who am I?

THE TANTRA TAPES

*I*t finally arrived: the day I would discover how my longtime obsession with sex could actually help me meditate. It was Friday, three days after I'd fallen in love with Nick. Other than that, it looked like any other day. Like Pavlov's pooch, I responded to the buzzing of my 6:30 a.m. alarm, then proceeded to shower, brush my teeth, and dress in my office casual best. I dried and combed my hair straight, rounded the tips with a curling iron, applied makeup with my right hand and perfume with my left. Next I slathered twin gobs of peanut butter and jelly over a slice of stale Ezekiel bread and devoured the front section of *The New York Times* while tonguing excess Jiff from the roof of my mouth, never questioning the habit of polishing my pearly whites before breakfast.

At eight o'clock on the dot, I swigged some OJ with my trusty Prozac, snatched up my purse, keys, and Blackberry, and was out the door. I raced to work in my red Ford Probe, ten miles over the speed limit (this to ensure time for my precious Starbucks run), pulling into the office parking lot at 8:29.

I kicked off work with a meeting to discuss the magazine status, returned phone calls and replied to emails until lunchtime, and wrote cover lines and my editor's letter over microwaved Kung Pao chicken, pebbly white rice, and an icy Diet Coke. By 2:00 p.m., I was then hyperventilating for no apparent reason. The main difference about this day was that my shortness of breath reminded me to call the ashram to reserve a seat for that evening's *satsang*, as part of my new commitment to relax and restrain my frantic mind a bit (and of course to see Nick again). I also dialed my Puerto Rican salsa partner to make sure he wasn't expecting to see me this Friday, thereby renewing (at least in my OCD mind) my commitment to born-again virginity.

Hanging up on my Latino lover's voicemail, I collapsed at my desk, fighting the numbing sensation of the antidepressants coursing through my blood. I just wanted to feel something—anything, dammit! I helped along the flood of tears that desperately wanted to flow by grabbing the emergency rosary beads stashed in my purse and whimpering out a few rounds of *Hail Mary* until I couldn't go on. When my head finally lifted up from my keyboard, I wondered if any of the "lasting happiness," "auspicious friendship," and "good luck" promised by the fortune cookie strips Scotch-taped across my monitor would ever actually manifest.

How much longer can this emotional roller coaster go on?

To lift the mood, I reread those fortunes to myself, playing the game of adding the words "in bed" to them as I nibbled on the remaining bites of chicken and rice:

You will find lasting happiness—in bed.

Your life will be blessed with auspicious friendship and good luck—in bed.

"Okay, make it so!" I said, crumpling my napkin and scoring a shot in the wastebasket a few feet away. The cheering section in my head went wild, offering a small adrenaline burst to spur me on through the afternoon's to-do list.

Fast forward to 9:00 p.m.

As soon as Nick gestured *namaste* with his hands to close Friday night's *satsang*, I made fists, celebrating my second successful meditation with a seated cabbage patch dance. After everyone else left their seats, he and I continued dialoging about a few basic spiritual principles, though not nearly enough for him to deduce anything *too* juicy about me and my sordid sex life. So then, had it been something in my meditation posture that gave it away?

Because when I stood up to leave, he silently handed me a set of Osho tapes entitled *Meditations on Tantra*. Up until that moment, I'd associated the word "tantra" with some kind of esoteric, church-forbidden style of sex in weird positions that I should never, under any circumstances, even envision, let alone try.

Well, never say never.

OMG, what just happened? I wondered as I stepped out the door, my sweaty palms clinging to the Tantra tapes. I had no idea who the twentieth-century Indian mystic Osho was and that I'd just been given a gift that would so exquisitely influence the rest of my life.

After my fairytale marriage gone awry and ensuing attempts at seeking satisfaction through orgasm, I admit that, secretly, I lived for sex. In fact, I worked, shopped, and breathed in anticipation of it. I couldn't get it off my mind. Yet, in that moment when Nick handed me the tapes, my mind stopped. Following that peaceful pause, my only conundrum was: *if this teacher was psychic enough to know these tapes would pique my curiosity, then why didn't he also know that I'd sworn my soul to born-again virginity?*

Why, oh why, had he given me these Tantra tapes? Did I look horny or something, like some wild, bug-eyed nymphomaniac? Did he also know that all my attempts to reconnect with my inner virgin were epic fails? Of course, I was also flattered that he'd selected them especially for me. *Did he find me so irresistible that he'd slash a vow of celibacy to indulge in mystical sex with me?* I was suddenly floating in the dream of being totally loved and appreciated by a man. A nice man. Or was he? *Maybe it was just like my father had said, that all men just wanted to fuck me, and that they couldn't give a shit about my inner beauty? A projection perhaps?*

I left meditation class dazed and confused, feeling simultaneously adored by and afraid of the man I'd turned to for sacred guidance. *What's a girl to do?* What else? Two weeks later, I married him, and he has since become my partner and best friend in life.

Hold on! Rewind...

I was alone on my drive home that night as the tapes rolled. They were difficult to understand because of Osho's accent. The feathery luster in his voice only made me want to listen closer. I could hardly believe my ears when I learned that Tantra is a philosophy, not an activity. He explained that it is about accepting life just as it is ... and if our minds aren't quiet enough to do that, like when I obsessed about sex and then judged myself for it, then Tantra even had techniques for transcending self-judgment by contacting our inner dimension *through* sex.

As my car's headlights illuminated the pitch-black open road before me, I talked back to the Osho tapes in my Marissa Tomei *My Cousin Vinny* voice: "Wait. Did you just say 'sex' is a means to acceptance, inner peace and self-forgiveness?!"

For me, sex and inner peace were not two ideas I'd *eva, eva woven togetha.* In fact, the sex I knew was anything but peaceful. It reverberated on high volume with outward moans and internal mental chatter questioning my every twitch and wiggle in bed. My inner dialogue went something like this: *Am I sexy? Am I beautiful enough for him? Am I doing enough to keep him wanting me again? Will he stay a while after we climax, or immediately pick up and leave me? And if he does leave, where will he go? Who else might he be hooking up with? Would he turn around come back for seconds? What else can I do to keep him running back for more? Do I have any more left to give?*

Sounds pathetic, but that's where I was at. Rock bottom. I'd compromised by overruling my inner voice, jeopardizing my life by placing myself in high-risk sexual situations to the point that something had to change. I knew the real answers could not be found in *Cosmo*, *Marie Claire*, or any other magazine. Up until I began exploring sex consciously through Tantra, I'd had no idea that sex could be such a truly uplifting experience; that sex, which had left me emotionally disappointed in the past, could transport me to new realms of lasting joy and fulfillment; that sex, which I'd once learned to fear and lust for equally, could actually be a vehicle for accessing the divine within and the voice of wisdom I so desperately wanted to heed, yet could barely hear through all the noise.

Conditioned by Western society, I was accustomed to a per-formance-oriented sexuality. In the United States, I was trained by television programming, magazines, and books to focus on pleasing my partner as The Goal rather than on cultivating sensu-ality and playfulness. Soon I recognized that my innate sensitivity had been numbed by an unspeakable pressure to not only make sure he orgasmed, but to make sure he believed he'd satisfied me like no other. This way he'd feel good about being with me and he wouldn't leave. If I could "control the situation" then maybe, just maybe, all the horror my father had prepared me for would not manifest.

Since separating from my ex, I had returned to the dating scene with a vengeance. I was only twenty-eight then but inside I felt old. I was wired and so tired from trying to design unique ways to pleasure a man and make sure he loved being in bed with only me, enough so that one day he would marry me and I'd never have to be alone. As such, I continued looking outward for signs—a smile, moan, hug, kiss, cuddle, bouquet of roses, risqué voicemail, or even a quick text—anything that implied he was thinking about me and was satisfied enough to keep me in his life.

Thanks to my new audiotapes, I became aware that—within a conscious relationship—the sex I craved could be used consciously to help me *feel* my inner being, my heart, my Self again. In that moment, I vowed to focus all my attention on exploring it. I soon would learn that my sexual rapport with Nick was not something taboo to be judged and repressed, but a doorway to discovering intimacy, loving union, and my true Self.

After my first spin through the Tantra tapes that fateful night, I heaved . . . a deep sigh of relief. I didn't have a bendy body, but I did have a flexible mind and open heart. And boy, was I ever ready to apply them!

And there it went again, my heart's enthusiasm running slightly ahead of my head—the first evidence that this "being aware of my thoughts" thing was starting to work.

Wait. Should I have sex with him yet? Does he lure all his unsuspecting victims into his web this way? Have the Tantra tapes been used on every young vixen that attended satsang? Was I the next sucker?

I proceeded with caution when I called him the next day to thank him and we made plans to meet for a walk on the beach. As much as I thought I should be *waaaay* freaked out, I wasn't. There were no words to describe the quality of presence with which Nick looked into my eyes. We had only met on Tuesday and our first discussion about becoming sexually active happened Saturday, the day after I'd listened to the Tantra tapes. Nick was supportive when I asked him to first go with me on an appointment for STD testing, during which I also planned to get on birth control, before we would begin.

But when I probed him about his sexual past, he offered more detail than I planned on.

I can handle it, at least this feels honest, I thought as he confirmed all of the references to his sexual history I'd read about in his bio on the ashram website. The write-up was making a point that he had reached dispassion through the many opportunities, sexual and otherwise, that life had presented him as a former collegiate and professional football player.

What? Okay, that's a kinda weird thing to mention in a bio, isn't it? His open-book character was magnetic to me. He really didn't care what people thought of him. I was also relieved that these deets were already online because it allowed me to open up dialogue, after the next *satsang*, when some of the ashram residents confirmed the fact that Nick—as sexually active as he'd been in his past—was not known to get involved with students.

"He hasn't been interested in anyone since I've known him," one of them said.

Another nodded in agreement. "If I were you, I wouldn't get my hopes up, though," he said. "He always tells us he is not into marriage."

When I asked Nick about this, he said, "That is true yet I am not against it either."

Reaching dispassion through a starter marriage and past sex with football groupies was a part of his history that I quickly came to accept and appreciate. Not because I loved envisioning it but because it allowed me to release every ounce of pent-up judgment about promiscuity. With that, I kissed the shame relating to my own sexcapades goodbye.

All those sweaty encounters had been part of what led us to this heart-to-heart.

"I knew, by the softness in your eyes, and by virtue of your even being able to walk into a class of this level, that you were ready for those tapes," he said.

If you would have told me then that Nick and I would go for STD testing and begin practicing Tantra within a week of meeting, I would not have believed it. I lovingly rib him every time the story comes up . . . of how my butt hole puckered and my face turned bright red when he told the clinician at Planned Parenthood, "We just met!"

The rib jab is just for fun, because shame is ancient history.

I'm Not a Body?!
Say It Isn't So

$\mathcal{U}$p to and even throughout the first three years of my marriage to Nick, I harbored a colossal fear of men. I'm certain it was born and festered in relationship to my father. The fear had followed me like a shadow, as I never could make intimate eye contact with my first husband without feeling like a six-year-old in a staring contest. And if a man looked me in the eyes—any man, even a teenage grocery bagger at the supermarket—I could not look back, let alone exchange a smile or pleasant hello. Instead, I'd stop breathing and fantasize about running in the opposite direction.

Meditation and Self-inquiry dissolved this deep-rooted fear of men. I remain grateful for one particular satsang, three months into our relationship, during which Nick conveyed wisdom to this effect:

> *We live in a universe of polarities where we cannot fully appreciate the experience of being a woman or a man without understanding and accepting the opposite sex.*

I chewed on that for three more months before arriving in India, where I committed to disidentify with my body, including its gender, so that I could awaken to who I truly am beyond the flesh. My contemplations led me to the understanding that all traits of a specific gender arise from the same divine Source. In my case, it was necessary to drop all concepts I'd accumulated in a patriarchal society where, in the shadows of "men" placed on pedestals, "women" appeared statistically less likely to realize their divinity. Jesus's disciples alone made the odds appear twelve to zero. Growing up Catholic, I had been raised to worship Jesus, whose sacred teachings I was now examining through the lens of non-duality using a Bible with Jesus's words printed in red. I also read *The Gospel According to Jesus* by Stephen Mitchell.[12] On top of that, I was devouring books by Ramana Maharshi, all the while receiving guidance from a male guru. The Women's Studies student in me deeply questioned this. Were there any female voices in the field of *Advaita Vedanta?*

Advaita Vedanta (literally "not two") is the Sanskrit word for nondualism; simply put, it is the idea that all is the Self, all is One, and nothing is separate from It. Advaitic studies challenged my every thought of distinction or division—and since thoughts seem to exist as distinct entities—it challenged every thought, including the root thought, *I!*

While in India I discovered the writings of a twentieth-century female sage, Anandamayi Ma, whom I at first rather shallowly related to because of her long, dark hair. As I read "her" teachings in the quiet corner of the District Central Library on Chengam Road in Tiruvannamalai, tears filled my eyes as it became quickly evident that the same Source had authored hers *and* Ramana's. With that insight, I blessed these elaborate male and female masks as tools by which I happily recognized that I am neither, while expressing as both in the play of life.

I mindfully returned the book to its spot on the shelf and met Nick near the library exit.

"So I *really* get that I'm not a woman and you're not a man!" I whispered.

He motioned for us to step outside onto the noisy road, where our conversation continued.

Functioning as the proverbial Oracle, he took the *jnana* to the next level by infusing the discussion with statements like, "Yes *and* if you wish to awaken, you must stop identifying with the flesh altogether." And "you are not a body, you are Existence itself" and "stop identifying with form; you are the formless Awareness!"

To say that this pissed me off at first would be an understatement. *Did he not notice that I had 'ears' that had heard all of this already?* Body and soul, I was rocked by the paradox of appearing to have a body and not veritably being one. Denial of this fact had recently spurred me to spend more money at Victoria's Secret than ever before.

In those early days of *sadhana,** contemplating "I am not only a body, I am also that which is not the body" briefly turned meditation into torture. Because when I thought I was a body, I took this personally. After twenty-eight years of roaming the planet convinced I was solely and soulfully a woman, this instruction to disidentify with my body through Self-awareness initially triggered an even deeper clinging to it.

Give this up?! Would it mean also giving up the pleasures of ice cream cake, the bliss of being massaged, the ecstasy of orgasm? Well, I was not ready to throw this baby out with the bathwater. *(Oh, and did I mention the soothing warmth of a lavender bubble bath?)*

Ah, but the holy taste of a margherita pizza, the tingly thrill of feathery touch, the sweaty joy of being kissed all over, caressed and made love with—these were not mine either, at least not quite in the way I'd imagined. I could suddenly relate to Cypher

---

* Sanskrit term for daily spiritual practice or discipline that leads to detachment from worldly things.

in *The Matrix*, who could not stop thinking about steak . . . when everything was at stake.

Suddenly everything I had ever been validated for—beauty, intelligence, hard work, and being the "nicest" person, my very identity—was rendered meaningless. And all things I was told I would be in the future—a good wife, a good mother—would I ever be able to play out those roles? Actually, what felt worst of all at the time was this: after nearly a lifetime of my father denying me miniskirts and my mother buying me minimizer bras, I'd finally summoned the courage to flaunt my curves in sexy clothes. So there I was, sitting in meditation, in my red lace push-up and matching flossy thong peeking out from my yoga pants, mounting the abyss between divorce and happily ever after with Mr. Right, and he was telling me *I am not a body, let alone a woman?*

WTF?

You see, I always, always, *always* listened to my teachers. I inherently trusted the ones I felt good around, and Nick was no exception. So I followed his instructions, looking for myself . . . eyes closed . . . with my inner eye . . . the *I* . . . the awareness, for the True Self that I had not yet recognized myself to be.

Shit! I was nowhere to be found in any organ, tissue, or cell.

Hot damn! I was cornered!

I didn't like not having answers for the teacher. It felt like I was dying.

So, what's a girl to do?

I . . . I . . . I . . . I'd make love with him and prove it wasn't true, or get enlightened trying.

Evidently, having been so deeply identified with my body, I needed to go to the extreme opposite of belief that I am not my body to somehow land in the middle and ultimately realize my oneness with the Infinite, which of course includes the body.

Didn't see that one coming!

THE KAMA-KAZE SUTRA

*B*efore finding Tantra, I had consumed *every* Kama Sutra book I could find, especially the gigantic hardcover editions with glossy photos, which I thumbed through nightly before flicking off my bedside lamp. Fueled by an insatiable sex drive, my visualizations were as crystalline as an Olympic athlete's. Every position was my favorite! I knew that this ancient tome of sex, and the juicy books based on it, must have worked just based on the number of people in India alone. It seemed conceivable that I too could become a master in the fine art of lovemaking. Squinting my freshly waxed brows, I studied those pictures as if to assimilate all the postures by osmosis. I'd rise like a phoenix, from the ashes of failed marriage, a twenty-first century winged Tantric-sex goddess like Isis!

I don't know how it happened, but I began using the terms Tantra and Kama Sutra interchangeably. Little did I understand how radically different they were. Only years later did I learn that the *Vatsyayana Kamasutra*, dating between 400 BCE and 300 AD,[13] is considered the oldest surviving Hindu textbook of erotic "love" (though I definitely wouldn't call it that now). What I didn't realize then is that it is full of lessons on "the art of living—about finding a partner, maintaining power in a marriage, committing adultery, living as or with a courtesan,* using drugs—and also about the positions in sexual intercourse." [14] Who knew? This is not to pass judgment on these things—just to say that, had I been aware of it at the time, I would not have swallowed sex advice from a source whose original chapter titles included "Reasons for Taking Another Man's Wife," "The Second-hand Woman," "The Wife Unlucky in Love," "Women Who Can Be Won Without Effort," "Testing Her Feelings," and "The Sex Life of a Man in Power." One chapter even instructs a repetitive slapping of the sternum between a woman's breasts during intercourse—and "if she protests, he strikes her on the head until she sobs." [15] *Wait, what?* Its directives continue further, painting a scene far from the picture of tenderness, love, and respect I was wanting. Needless to say, when I learned this, it aroused nothing but my inner feminist.

Alas, lust is blind, sex sells, and the books I'd read about Kama Sutra offered little to no historical context; they were all about naked bodies in pleasure-enhancing positions. So there I lay between my silky white sheets under the hypnosis of it all, barely skimming the captions under the pictures, never mind bothering to query the source of this user's manual for sex offenders. Even if hypothetically the objective were to invoke surrender, it still seems to miss the essential distinction between spiritual surrender through love and being brutally pummeled into submission. Granted, some of the positions appeared to promote intimacy, given the teamwork required to bend and coil bodies into them, but *what brand of intimacy . . . exactly? And at what cost?* If only I'd been aware of this sooner, I would have been conscious enough to not place myself in painful positions, physically and emotionally, during my year of promiscuity between marriages.

---

* A prostitute, especially one with upper-class clients.

As I later found out, in contrast to the physical basis of the Kama Sutra, Tantra is the lover's path of devotion and spiritual surrender. It is neither a religion nor a commercialized yoga, but rather the opposite of these because its philosophy frees you from dogma, encouraging you to trust your own experience and perceptions. Where sex is concerned, Tantra utilizes it as an affectionate foray to meditation.

To simplify, authentic Tantra has two primary components: sensitivity and awareness. The intention is to increase these in all areas of life, not just in the bedroom, though sex becomes a sacred practice through which both are cultivated and strengthened. Meditative witnessing as sexual tension builds and releases (without releasing all the way) allows you to float upon the crest of orgasm. The primary focus is to sustain the orgasm in a state of relaxed alertness. In this way, there is a series of builds and releases without an orgasm or ejaculation, rather than the more common single build with one intensified release. Awareness of the tension-release cycle allows you to identify the mechanism of desire that is part and parcel of physical existence. Breath is another tension-release cycle. Holding your breath after an exhale brings your awareness to the natural desire to take another breath; and when your awareness is noticing itself, it is impossible to have another thought. All of life is a cycle; tension and release are found most everywhere when one becomes increasingly present. In tantric lovemaking, thought-free intervals that occur during Tantric orgasm provide glimpses of pure Being.

The cosmic joke is ever tickling the Tantric lovers, who pursue carnal intimacy only to realize that these glimpses of Oneness do not "happen" because of something they've done, sexually or otherwise. It grows clear that riding the waves of tension-release cycles is aligning with the ultimate Truth. To exist *as* this natural flow requires the letting go of all self-definitions and restrictions, resulting in the submission of the "me-thought." Indeed, it was Tantra that led my inner wild horse to the waters of this ultimate understanding. Embracing sex as a meditation and not just as a means of satisfying bodily impulses, I entered the ocean of bliss and realized I was one with It, and I am never actually separate from It.

As a practical matter of functioning in the world, I had to shake off my fear of what people would think of the book publisher who writes and speaks publicly about meditation and Self-inquiry interspersed with sexuality.

Would anyone want to associate with me anymore?

Respected doctors, dentists, lawyers, and media professionals who attended my earliest talks on Tantra in the cramped back rooms of spiritual bookstores told me that what I had to say was not only important but supremely essential in life. Now I was not clothed in traditional sex-ed credentials like Dr. Ruth, yet for whatever reason I had something to convey about sexuality—something people from all walks of life could resonate with. Whatever the questions, answers flowed from my experience, drawing audiences closer, and so often I wondered to myself, *God, how on earth did I end up doing this?*

Around the time I started sharing Tantra publicly in 2006, a cable television show aired on the topic. When I heard about it, my heart leapt. *Would it expose the masses to this precious path of Love and transcendent awareness?* But its portrayal of "tantra" as an orgy could not have been further from my experience where the only apparent threesome is between two lovers and God—until all appearances dissolve into timeless Oneness. If one were to be with more than one lover at a time, it would introduce the element of time as attention ricochets among one's lovers and oneself. This is where one would have to look within—is it possible to pay full attention to more than one thought (or in this case, lover) at a time?

And while one's body is physically engaged with one lover and another who is present, is one's sense of attention in any way pulled by the sense of a third party?

In private sessions, Nick and I met with a number of couples who had been to such workshops, identified as polyamorous, or were involved in the swingers' lifestyle, and expressed concerns that their relationships were not progressing toward deeper intimacy. With them we shared the metaphor of having multiple lovers being like digging five holes, each ten feet deep rather than one hole fifty feet deep. We also asked them, "Could this be an egoic strategy to avoid intimacy and vulnerability in the relationship?" For most, these were not comfortable conversations. And those who looked within for answers witnessed the dissolution of their fears.

The number of lovers any one person feels drawn to be with is a karmic matter that can only be resolved within. When seeking to practice Tantra, the key is to pair with someone who is as devoted to their spiritual practice as you are, and to then utilize the "other" as a doorway to transcend the sense of separation. This surrender occurs when you can be your authentic Self with them and trust that they will not judge, reject, or attempt to hurt you even when life situations inevitably get uncomfortable. Then, you can be vulnerable, and so can they. And it is during this surrender that the door to the Infinite opens when you least expect it.

It has often been said that sexual energy is the most powerful known force on earth. That is because there is so much energy moving into people's constricted sex centers that it is simply overwhelming to them. In fact, some philosophies postulate that human psychoses are rooted in sexual suppression, resulting in tension and confusion. Is it any wonder that modern psychology is based on Freud's observation that people's basic instincts toward sex have been repressed in the name of living a "civilized life"? It is no surprise that this father of psychoanalysis advised humanity:

"Look into the depths of your own soul and learn first to know yourself, then you will understand why this illness was bound to come upon you and perhaps you will thenceforth avoid falling ill."[16]

While I'm not an advocate of Freudian psychoanalysis per se, in this case his words do point to the solution. Looking into the depths of your soul and first knowing your Self, is in fact, the whole point of the spiritual journey. If you know all that there is to know, but you don't know the knower, then what can you possibly know?

Prior to my embarking on the Tantric journey, my sexuality was 100 percent friction-based. Yet this tension-release cycle proved physically addictive, fueling an obsession with sex and the pursuit of orgasmic pleasure. To this day, the prevalence of pornography and sex-focused advertisements merely reflects a world wherein love and lasting happiness seem perpetually "just out of reach" because people seek them exclusively in the gross physical dimension.

One of the differences in the manner that Nick and I present Tantra, in contrast with many other "tantric" schools of thought, relates to their promotion of arousal and genital excitation. We don't focus on arousal or excitation because intentional clitoral and penile stimulation pinches off the rise of *kundalini* (energy) to the higher centers associated with Self-realization. What we must understand is: Tantric bliss is not that of your traditional peak orgasm involving isolated stimulation of the genitals, yet as the orgasm hovers just below the threshold of climax, it allows for a sustained "near-peak" orgasm where the mind is held still with the door to the Divine wide open. Some believe that a sub-climactic orgasm is inferior to reaching the top of the mountain via a peak burst. Yet consider that most orgasms usually last only seconds, whereas the sub-peak (or valley) orgasm, when practiced consciously, can be sustained for many hours on end. Yes, you heard right! ☺

With Tantra, orgasm is transcendental, utilizing the body to focus attention toward the inner realm, the higher consciousness that defies all mental and physical conceptions. Or, as Jesus called it, "the peace that passeth all understanding." Here, senses heighten and fall away to a palpable sense of sublime Oneness with all existence. Nick and I call it the "Heart orgasm." It is an experience of orgasm that paradoxically dissolves the quest for experience. The thought *"I'm cumming"* is no longer present, as the "I" (the experiencer) and the orgasm (the experience) have become one by combining into *the experiencing* and all that remains is the blissful awareness, or divine ecstasy.

Ahhhhh, yet these are mere words—you just have to try it! And when the opportunity arises to practice making love in this manner, remain open to the possibility of something more satisfying than anything you have ever known, as the Heart orgasm exceeds the localized genital orgasm, exponentially.

During the years following the aforementioned cable TV version of tantra, mainstream yoga magazines and websites were portraying what they dubbed the Neo-Tantra Movement. Even when intelligent articles were available to read, the same publications advertised workshops where attendees participated in tantric exercises that often encouraged multiple partners simultaneously. One would also find sex-toy ads sponsoring websites claiming to teach Tantra; yet again it was my experience that plastic sex toys masquerading as human flesh served only to callous and numb the vaginal tissues and nerve endings, diminishing vital sensitivity! The world was seeing facets of a pseudo-tantric path unlike the authentic path that is available.

At play in the paradox, our website OpenHeartTantra.com was not sex-centric, but that did not stop the influx of phone calls from men and women whose inquiries reflected the worldly interpretation of Tantra. Even though it was clearly stated that Nick and I are monogamous and that participants would remain fully clothed during instructional sessions, the propositions poured in: What exactly would we do with them sexually? What would be the extent of the physical contact? And what kinds of positions would they learn? To which I'd reply, "Tantra is not about learning positions—it is about dropping your positions."* It is an attitude toward life, not a ritual or posture that eventually comes to an end. It is not the Kama Sutra but the Kama-kaze Sutra—where you intentionally die to the illusion of what you thought you were, only to be reborn as your ultimate potential.

Tantra was invaluable in lifting the veils that had once prevented me from accessing my own inner being and intuition. This interior realm to which Tantra led was of course not a physical one, but ethereal. Before making love each time, we meditated. Not like stock-art photos of couples meditating on the beach with their spines aligned and hands in mudras; we often sat still in our own chairs for about ten minutes, and only when we felt ready did we open our eyes and undress ourselves or each other, while keeping attention turned inward toward Self-awareness.

We always confirmed whether a conscious communication was necessary before engaging physically, to ensure we arrived in each other's embrace relaxed and clear of any upset that may have arisen earlier. Yes, this meant that, even if I'd planned on a Tantric-sex evening, it occasionally turned into a lengthy conscious communication minus lovemaking.†

This was the opposite of the "just dive in the sack" standard in my previous relationships. Approaching lovemaking patiently and with presence taught me to value sex in a whole new light. I never again took it for granted, or saw it as a fringe benefit I

---

* Here "positions" refers to mental positions, all linked to the need to be right.
† See "Love Listens" in Part Four for details on conscious communication.

was entitled to as somebody's girlfriend or spouse. My desire to explore sex Tantrically incentivized me to prioritize living in a state of allowing, which made all the times that I arrived like a clear river in his arms feel precious and perfect.

And from there with slim to no verbal communication and in no particular order, we often feather-touched each other's skin, kissed, breathed, listened to each other's heartbeat, lay in spoon position with his penis pressed against my sacrum, and practiced breast-massage. All this time, I focused on consciously observing that each phenomenon—a drop of sweat, my skin, chills rushing up my spine, shoulders, neck, ears, heat, Nick's breath, his penis entering *me*—was a thought *in me*. I practiced Self-awareness continuously. If pain arose, I communicated it and it was received with compassion and slowing down. Sometimes we sustained eye contact upon entry, though more often than not, I felt my eyelids fluttering closed and rested there. In this timeless dimension, free from thought, I was far from a once self-diagnosed nymphomaniac with my perfumed, negligéed body braided with my lover's, hips thrusting to instigate multiple rounds of sex. In fact, it was there, in sustained states of quiescent bliss, that I came to forgive my body-mind for what she saw as her sins and honor that expression of myself as a protective costume I wore along the path of realizing I am vastly more.

Though sexuality is an element of the Tantric path, it is merely a door. I found Tantra most transformative when I did not get stuck in the doorway of lust or arousal. Once I began approaching sex more meditatively, the need to explode lost its grip as my attention was drawn more and more toward a relaxation implosion. That is not to say that I did not feel pleasure; I most certainly did, but pleasure was not the primary focus. Relaxed awareness had become the Holy Grail.

High-Octave Orgasm

On a late fall afternoon in my sophomore year of high school, my father caught me making out with my senior boyfriend in the driveway. The neighbor's son who usually drove me home from marching band practice had been absent from school that day. When I whipped out my hitchhiking thumb and asked my Romeo for a lift, I didn't realize that my retired father was two steps ahead and waiting.

With eyes only for each other, my man and I were oblivious to our private voyeur—The Dad. Our lips were locked in the space above the console of his Saturn. Between Styx's "Come Sail Away" streaming from the radio and his hands caressing my breasts, the thrill of this rare occasion had me orgasming in my gym shorts. My father must have raised the garage door sometime between when we parked and when our passionate kiss lingered toward its ill-fated end. When my eyes slowly opened, I noticed the door on its way down but thought little of it, my tingling body riding a pleasure high that carried me into the house.

Right after setting down my purse, flute case, and backpack, I approached my mother for a hug and kiss. She stopped me sheerly by the look in her eye. "Bad news," she said, her face white with shock, as if someone had died moments earlier. "Your father saw everything and he does not want to lay eyes on you for two solid weeks or ... or he will kill you."

As my gut clenched, my heart raced, and my body started to tremble, I could find no refuge from fear, not even in my mother's momentary embrace.

"You'd better go to your room," she whispered in my ear. "And I mean it—*do not* let him see you because I don't know what he will do."

For a fortnight, I lived with the fright that my father was going to murder me. The thought that *experiencing pleasure makes me bad* had taken root. From that point forward, I hesitated to express enjoyment of sensual pleasure and did whatever I could to skirt the O-word in conversations, even when my bestie tried to pinky-swear secrets out of me wanted to compare notes about our orgasmic experiences. I imagine this is why God led me to the path of awakening through orgasm—to heal from deep-rooted shame and sexual trauma and share the wisdom of authentic Tantra in service to humanity.

It was Easter Sunday before church when I was just eight years old. Following my a.m. binge on marshmallow Peeps, jelly beans, and chocolate bunny ears, I sat on the piano bench dressed in my Sunday best: ruffled, powder-blue and white polka-dot dress, brown locks curled and pulled up into a tight ponytail, white stockings, and even whiter patent leather Mary Janes. My feet dangled from the wooden bench, as my legs were too short even for my tippy toes to reach the pedals. Poised to practice Haydn's "Gypsy Rondo," which I'd no doubt be performing for my relatives later, I arched my fingers above the keys and just then . . . a sudden throb in my most private part. Attempting to ignore it, I closed my eyes to play from memory and began tickling the ivories, which seemed to help this most pleasurable pulsing sensation along until it faded with the final chord, leaving me all tingly. Silent, I sat in the holiest of spaces, bathed in goose bumps, until my little brother barreled down the stairs to the familiar jingle of my mother's car keys. It was time for church.

In retrospect, I am not surprised that my very first orgasm occurred in the midst of a clear-minded artistic expression. This naturalness and relaxation allowed me to sense pure life energy flowing through my body, even in the thick of an angst-ridden childhood. With no words for what had just occurred, and no thought that it would ever happen again, I felt simply showered in sweetness. Soon other people began fading back in to my reality, and there was a world again.

This world did have a name for what had happened, and in my teens it fueled my compulsion to experience it often . . . if not continuously! The more magazine articles I read about how to achieve an orgasm, the harder I tried. In fact, I dove pelvis first into one romance after another, with my goal being to experience as much pleasure as possible without actually having to sacrifice my virginity. Orgasm became the prize I could win every time, as long as I grinded hard enough through my blue jeans or trusted my lover's hands enough to take me there. Because I'd come to gauge my worth and desirability as a woman on how wild I could be in the boudoir, my self-esteem tanked when the orgasms stopped in my mid-twenties and I found myself faking them. Despite the clouds of confusion that had rolled in during my first marriage, I approached sex enthusiastically with the hopes that it could help restore physical and emotional closeness. When it didn't, I blamed myself for all that went wrong in the bedroom, and outside of it too. Deeper down the shame pit I sank, as if into quicksand.

∞

Until I discovered Tantra, society's standard messaging prevailed that bodies were the source and cause of orgasmic bliss and that "I" had to do something outrageous to reach orgasm. Yet my marriage with Nick revealed that sex could be approached as a meditation and creative expression of love, reviving the possibility of orgasm as an effortless unfoldment.

When I conceived of orgasm in the old way, it had been a business transaction: *I'll satisfy him once he satisfies me, or if he satisfies me first, then I'll owe him one.* It became an object of lust, and so fear was always there too. *Would it happen or not? Would I have to fake it?* Would my lover be pleased or look elsewhere? This constant tension pinched off my vitality, corking it in my lower back at the sex center. The dam busted often in a localized release, especially when induced by high-friction foreplay and intercourse. In my experience, the temporal nature of a localized orgasm created desire for another, each time requiring additional tension to create a comparable release. This tendency prevented the experience of heart-centered orgasm experienced as divine union.

When inner awareness became my primary focus rather than achieving orgasm, everything changed. Bliss wasn't meant to be an isolated event like that one time after band practice—it was a life-affirming state of being that I could tap into and embody at any time. All of the sexual confusion that I'd toted with me since my teens dissolved in the inquiry: *Who is aware of the orgasm?*, awakening, within me, the high-octave orgasm.

SEX SEEN

*O*nce upon a time, the word *sex* invoked visions of silk sheets, lace negligées, and swollen genitalia thirsting for orgasm, not to mention obsession with how succulent my body looked and my partner's too. Now I laugh because when my editor friend asked me to write a Tantric sex scene for this book, the first image that popped to mind was the dusty streets of Tiruvannamalai, India.

Envision a sea of honking buses bursting with passengers hanging out windows, co-existing with scooters zipping through waves of orange-clad swamis, spiritual seekers, and women in bright saris carrying baskets and children in their arms, balancing jugs on their heads with marigold garlands in their hair. On these roads, all flows in harmony with the horned bulls crossing the road perpendicular to traffic and the honey-bee buzz of motor rickshaws weaving through it all. Here, jasmine flowers and sacred incense mix with burning trash on alleyways lit by pearly smiles of roadside merchants luring passersby to sample chai and bananas or run fingers over prayer beads and exotic textiles. Beggars kneel open-palmed beneath tattered movie posters stuck to cement walls that feature mostly men's sunglassed faces ogling the occasional woman fully clothed. The crowds of people ambling through this scene is the only implication that sex indeed happens here.

Ubiquitous sensory stimuli is a regular day at the office under India's blazing winter sun. And yet amidst it all one thing stood out to me above all else—it was the people's sweet surrender radiating softly through their eyes. This made such an impression on me that, after my first day ever walking on the sacred hill of Arunachala, I wrote in my journal dated December 8, 2004:

There is no fear in their eyes.

What a curious thing to notice, *no fear*. What had made fear the barometer with which I measured the light in people's eyes?

Meditation on Arunachala had revealed the threads of duality still knotted together as my *fear of pain*. At that point, I dreaded the pain of catching flak for my life decisions, yet that was only secondary to my resistance to pain in the realm of sex. I wanted sex so badly, I actually feared the pain of not having it. I feared the pain of what living without sex could mean—that I was unworthy, unwanted, unwelcome in a lover's arms. And I feared the physical pain of intercourse. Gentle as Nick was, I'd feel a hot, piercing sensation when his penis pressed against a certain point inside that made me want to scream. Up to that point, I'd suppressed it and thus feared knowing that I'd pant and push through it, taking on the weight of this agony to avoid the emotion beneath it.

No one else would ever have to know how much it hurt. No one else would have to relive my daunting childhood memories or fight my inner war with the gag reflex. No one else would have to embody my anguish, compounded during college by way of vacant moans and the scent of sweat, alcohol and smoke, the abandonment in darkness, and the tearful choke of waking up all alone, only to seal the humiliation with the dreaded cross-campus walk of shame. I feared facing this pain more than anything in the world. But I knew it was necessary if I ever wished to attain the freedom I'd glimpsed in these Indian people's eyes.

I'd made the passage to India alongside Nick and with a group of other students participating in a six-week intensive Self-inquiry immersion program. Together we resided in the Mountain Breeze, a three-story home on Ramana Nagar Street. Nick and I shared the first-floor bedroom, which had its own bathroom attached, luxurious when compared with the rooms shared by my classmates above us.

Nestled beneath a bright-yellow Indian bedspread, I cherished waking up every morning as roosters sang and the light streamed in through the barred, mosquito-screened windows. I dressed in my pink Punjabi suit, respectfully chosen to blend in and cover all of the flesh I was accustomed to revealing back in the United States. As I disrobed one particular afternoon to take a siesta, I knew that nap time could very well lead to lovemaking. Quite unlike me, I was not in the mood. My stomach was unsettled on account of local water that had snuck undetected into my mixed-berry smoothie via crushed ice; plus, I was still cranky from jet lag. But. As soon as I felt Nick's warm, naked body spoon-in under the covers, his penis settling along my sacrum, his arms encircling my shoulders, and the belly of his palms settling gently on my breasts, nap time was officially over.

As our bodies became one, our tender union did not trigger a tsunami of past memories or pull my mind out of the moment this time. Being so far away from everything familiar, I was particularly present. Our tantric lovemaking often releases buried emotional scars and today would be no exception. The promise of transcendental pleasure provided me all the incentive I needed to be brave and face that searing pain.

As Nick's penis pressed against *the spot*, the memory of being sexually abused by my father surfaced with a shrill shriek that made me want to cover my own ears, but there was no avoiding it now. Nick maintained a supportive stillness. For a moment I wondered, *will anyone come to check on me?* No, nothing. My mind turned inward as the Self-inquiry began unfurling on its own.

Can I accept that this pain is happening?

A calm *yes* arose in me.

Who is aware of it?

I am.

Who am I?

Suddenly the pain faded and *pfft*, it was gone. No words were exchanged with Nick in the midst of this Self-inquiry—only a deep gaze. We were void of expectation to stay locked in a stare or say anything, for what is there to say during such exquisite peace?

But maybe *someone* had heard my cry. Because . . .

Mooooooo . . .

"Holy . . ." I said. "Is there a cow outside the window?!"

Mooooooo . . .

Yup, I thought, *that's a cow.*

"Penelope," Nick whispered, "are you sure you want to turn outward?"

"*Nooooooo . . .*" I smiled and returned inward.

It was true. In this lucid state of awareness, the moo was seen as a mere distraction, no matter how peculiar it is to have a cow saunter fifteen feet of where one is making love. I sunk inward again, only deeper this time. Every instance of pain that I'd ever spun a story about was seen as equivalent to this *mooooooo* of my sacred friend.

This is not to diminish the experience of pain, but to acknowledge that, in its essence, it is just a *moooo*vement in consciousness. Pain proved only another ripple when all was seen to be the ocean of consciousness.

Soon the mooing subsided and when I opened my eyes, Nick was still there gazing at me, and I wondered . . .

Who is thinking that?

Because I could not vouch that there was even a "him" in that body looking out.

Nick, my beloved, was a thought.

Once sex too was seen as just a thought, the fear of pain and obsession with it slipped off as easily as my panties. I then came to redefine and recognize sex as a powerful tool for transcendence.

As our bodies lay entangled, I saw a look in Nick's eyes that I'd never seen before—a mirror of my own recognition that I was awake.

Soon it was time to return to the hill for an evening walk, followed by a veggie pizza dinner at one of our favorite rooftop cafes. It was time to wrap a sari around my sacred temple and step once again into the streets of India. Only this time—*no fear*. I'd wink at the cow who almost turned me outward. I'd feel the bustle on the streets closer than my own pulse. I'd hear the honking buses as my own laughter. I'd smell the savory aromas as my own breath. And thanks to my afternoon of sex seen, I'd see my own love shining through the eyes of everyone.

When I Caught the Bouquet

Today is the day
Fate took my hand
in a way
I at first
didn't quite
understand

As we danced across the ocean
my heart flooded with the notion
endless surprises lie on the horizon
just not in a way I can lay eyes on

After all this spinning in circles
I'd landed on the shore of Trust
witness to the wedding
of my faith and my will
the band playing on
to the tune of
Be Still

When I caught the bouquet
of mist, diamonds and clay
it passed right through my hand
and merged with
the sea, sand and sky

Today is the day
Destiny held me
forever in sight
just as I Am,
at one with
the Light

PART THREE

Committing to Love

THE WISDOM OF INTERDEPENDENCE

*W*hat does it look like to commit to a relationship and remain free? For me, this was *the* question. As happy as a couple appeared from my perspective, how could I know if both partners felt free? To know that, I'd have to perceive life through the eyes of those people—and since I could only see through my own eyes, the search for a definition of freedom would have to begin with me.

On the morning after my first meditation, the phone rang at about 11:30 in my office. It was Nick. He asked me to dinner that night, but I couldn't go due to a previously scheduled date with a coworker—which felt like a business appointment compared to the prospect of an intimate evening with the new and mysterious Nick. Yet I was never the kind of girl who broke her agreements, even though this time I wanted to.

"Tonight I have plans, but how about some other time, soon?" I said.

"Sure," he said. "That would be nice."

"I'll see you Friday at *satsang*," I said.

After hanging up, a tidal wave of anxiety crashed over me. You could say I had more than a date that evening. I had a plane ticket to visit yet a different man across the country the next weekend. I was also sporting brand-new baggage over last week's split with Adonis, a broken heart over the lover in New York (who hadn't called me in three days), two missed calls from my salsa partner, and one voice message from my not-quite-yet-ex-husband asking me to reconsider. Is it any wonder I needed to learn meditation?

To avoid the lingering jitters from having spread my legs and myself so thin among prospective lovers, I distracted myself with job stress. While editing article after article about addiction, I took in more than the recommended daily dose of thoughts about "codependency." Ignoring its specific clinical meaning, I blanket-diagnosed myself as codependent. I rationalized this label because I was struggling to break free of guilt for leaving my marriage—and now apparently my ex "needed" me the minute I committed to ending my emotional dependence on him or anyone for that matter. It seemed the antidepressants and weekly counseling sessions were the only things holding me together as I came unwound.

I needed an intervention—a divine intervention. I spent most evenings alone at Barnes & Noble, pacing the aisles, waiting for my phone to ring. At one point in the fog of it all, I abandoned the psychology aisle for the spiritual section, where I began to notice different books with a recurring message: "Love is surrender." *But how could this be, when it so sharply contradicted my therapist's mantra: "Do not lose yourself in a relationship"?*

Now that I'd fallen in love with Nick, what on earth was I supposed to do? Through my efforts to murder codependency and love myself with meditation, all I knew was that I'd completely lost it this time—it being my sense of self. Given the passion our togetherness stirred, it had been impossible not to. He showed up fifteen minutes early for our first date, abolishing any luxury of my last-minute preparations like makeup, perfume, and pillow-straightening, which I'd believed mandatory for landing Mr. Right. The fact that he cared about me anyway, paying no attention to such superficialities, sucked me into the vacuum all the more . . . oh my.

To make matters better, he was okay with the PDA—not my "personal digital assistant" as we called our cell phones in those days—yes, public displays of affection. On my lunch breaks, he hoisted me up and whisked me through the doors of Taco Bell past the hot-sauce counter into the ordering line, as if waltzing me off to bed on our wedding night. At the grocery store, he impelled me to ballroom-style dance in the cereal aisle. On the checkout line, other customers smirked as he tore open a pack of cherries and fed them to me one by one, until my embarrassment dissolved into hysterical laughter. I'd been caught off guard again! *Exactly what was it about people looking at me funny that I had been afraid of all my life?* Surrounded by tabloids, I found myself cornered into making the most vital decision of my life: which mattered more, what people thought of me, or living a life filled with passion and love?

Letting go of caring what other people thought was a skeleton key to the mysterious surrender that opened the door to love. What could be more liberating than loving myself enough to be who I am and embracing the freedom to consciously fulfill my desires? Blame it on my birth chart but with my whole being, I had craved romance with a monogamous partner. I had *wanted* to fall head-over-heels in love. I no longer felt balanced when subjecting myself to the scrutiny of outside sources. Since they weren't tangoing in my flip-flops, how could they ever truly know my best interests? Right there in the grocery store, I'd learned to trust life like never before.

Certainly, my faith was tested in the months to come. The withering momentum of beating myself up inside for past codependent behaviors did not come to an end overnight. Even while severing ties with my therapist and the other men, I found myself drawn back to the pages of codependency books. A little devil on my shoulder desperately warned that I needed such books in case Nick turned out like the rest.

But one day in meditation, my inner voice asserted itself ever so gently:

> *Enough of this nonsense! Let yourself feel attraction, and desire, and whatever else you are feeling. To be against feeling anything is a prison.*
>
> *P.S. You could not encounter this wisdom were it not time to know the truth.*

I got the message—the time had come to face my fear of codependency once again. Upon vowing to enter this relationship completely naked and vulnerable, I stopped blaming myself for past foolishness. Because who doesn't want love? The longing for a lover's touch is visceral, and what being, believing their happiness to be wrapped up in it, would not give up anything and everything for it? My previous escapades had been testament to that. Yet through it all, I learned that the very process of looking outside myself for love had assured me of not finding it. All effort to attain it had only pushed it further away.

I'd been given another chance at love, and this time I wasn't gonna blow it. There was no time for worrying that I could screw it up, and no time for labeling myself "codependent" and perpetuating another cycle of "attach" and "break up." Through meditation on the *I* thought, it was revealed in my heart that love does not require two people to feel it, just one. The energy of codependent attachment had not disappeared, but was transmuted into a unifying recognition of the interdependence of me and my lover . . . and all of life. Simply by practicing Self-inquiry.

Who is this I that searches for love?

It's me.

And if I am aware of this "me" objectively, can it be who I really am?

Peace . . . until my therapist's words came back to haunt me: "Do not lose yourself in a relationship."

But who was this self she was addressing?

Was it the same sense of "me" now being questioned?

Had my therapist been talking to an impostor all this time?

And that's how I came to the conclusion that the only "me" that can ever get lost in a relationship is the ego-sense of me, the little self that once posed as my True Self. When I became aware as my True Self, who else was left to depend on?

TEACHER, LOVER, HUSBAND, FRIEND

*M*y therapist frowned when I told her that Nick and I were married within two weeks of meeting. "So fast?" she challenged. To her, this was reckless behavior. To me, it was destiny.

On a dinner date during our first two weeks together, I asked Nick about his reported lack of interest in marriage. Awash in the bliss of newfound love, I was not fishing for his hand in it. Being the good student of life I was, my divorce had led me to question the purpose of institutionalized marriage. Our dinner conversation sounded like two old hippies, relentlessly questioning "The Man." *What did two people need a certificate or witnesses for, if they were truly in love? Wouldn't that just signify a lack of trust somewhere? Shouldn't your spouse be your best friend? Do you ever need a contract for a friendship? What recourse would they need if they were absolutely committed to accepting each other exactly as they are?*

Our banter cut through my conditioning like a hot knife through the cheesecake we shared for dessert. I was surprised (and a bit proud of myself) for not feeling the need to get legally married ever again either.

On the drive home, Nick said, "But if I were going to be married again, I'd want it to be with you."

Maybe it was the way he said it, but it felt like the nicest thing anyone had ever said to me.

∞

In the privacy of my bed the next morning, with no legal officiant in sight, Nick said, "Will you marry me?"

I said, "Yes!" And that was it, no ceremony, only a tender, loving reception in each other's arms. We agreed that, from that point forward we were married, and celebrated with breakfast at our favorite bagel shop.

Nick and I were sauntering hand-in-hand toward his Honda Rebel motorcycle in a parking lot in our old hometown of Coral Springs, our stomachs full of coffee, pumpernickel, and cream cheese. Dead in the middle of the busy traffic aisle, he stopped abruptly, turned to me, and asked, "If you had to choose, would you rather I be your teacher or your husband?"

I was confused, since we were already married.

"Hmmm," I pondered, but only for a second before my final answer slipped through my lips faster than the speed of thought. "My teacher."

As much as it surprised me, I was certain of it. I had exhausted my body and mind on failed romances. I couldn't bear the thought of another one. Spiritual truth had now become my priority and first love. I knew I'd been led to Nick as a teacher for that very reason. In reality, the one we marry is always our teacher, yet the degree of intellectual pride with which I entered this union required my spouse to be a conscious teacher so I wouldn't run when the ego was under squeeze.

Guiding us out of the way of an oncoming car with his cat-like reflexes, he smiled. "I am just interested in your priorities."

Our two-week courtship had been blissful as I skydanced through my days and we made love each night, yet now the real inner journey was afoot.

My priorities? What were my priorities?

Realizing my connection with God was definitely priority one. Initially, this was synonymous with turning inward. Unless I was working "on purpose" within scheduled time blocks, I needed to literally turn away from mirrors, media, computers, and my phone, toward the inner body and formless dimension of meditation. My meditation practice increased my sensitivity, leading to my next priority: experiencing my feelings without judging them. Living in accordance with these priorities carved a space where honesty reigned. And once I deliberately witnessed my changeable emotional states, I noticed areas where I was not being honest with myself.

It seemed that, when Nick was not massaging my back, he was rubbing my every nerve with constant questions about whether I was practicing Self-inquiry. *Please could we just cook or shower or pump gas—anything—without a mention of the word "presence" or "inquiry"? No, I'm not annoy . . . ugh. Why do you joke about how much I talk but you keep asking me questions? Like, this is the way I learned to peel garlic and I don't care if yours is more efficient, mine's not wrong!* The "nicest person" ribbon awarded to me in first grade was coming apart at the seams. "You are so sweet!" people had said to me all my life. Yet as my buttons got pushed, it threw my sugar and spice out the window. The more I watched myself react nicely, the more I realized being excessively nice all the time was not actually a virtue but a dishonest act, a learned behavior to help me feel safe in what I had perceived as a threatening world.

This personality pattern came to a head during our second trip to Tiruvannamalai in December of 2005. Having walked about the locale the previous year, we decided to rent bicycles this time. Only the bike I was given was not my lightweight, ten-speed Schwinn. Being a woman's model suitable for riding in a sari, it had a low crossbar; and its heavy handlebars, fitted with a gargantuan basket, made it difficult to steer. It took some getting used to and by the time I worked up enough moxie to enter the DIY "bike lane" on the far left side of the bustling main road toward Sri Ramana Ashram, Nick and my friends were way ahead and almost out of sight. I pedaled and swerved left, pedaled and swerved right, in a futile but frantic attempt to catch up. Everybody else took to their bikes like eagles to flight and appeared to even be *enjoying* the ride abreast honking traffic, hordes of people, and road dust in the air. But I, I was not having fun. At all. And just when my throat was beginning to swell and tears had almost pushed their way up and out, a big, brown bus—I mean a Greyhound-size puppy with open windows and more people hanging out than should be legal—went *hooooooooooonnnnnnnkkkk* and came within inches of crushing me under its tires!

That was it. I was going to lie bloody and dying right there, in the streets of sacred India.

I squeezed back on the foot brakes, jumped off the bike, let it fall to the side of the road, and screamed at the top of my lungs. "I Ammmmmmmmm!" I shouted for Nick as I watched him shrink into a tiny dot on the horizon. Rickshaws, saris, jasmine petals, barefoot children, women with water buckets on heads, bananas, papayas, smoke, moneys, motorbikes, marigolds, rice-powder mandalas, cows, brooms, babies, dogs—everyone, everything—except Nick, who had left me there to die. I knew there was no way he was going to hear me calling his name on that street.

I watched a mass drove of Indian people—heavy and skinny, young and old, high caste and low caste—gather around me. I continued to cry and yell "I Ammmmmmmmm!" at the top of my lungs—not out of fear anymore, but sheer anger that I'd been left behind and almost squashed under a bus.

Nick must have turned back to check on my whereabouts because the next thing I knew, he was pedaling toward me. When he got within five feet of me, I let him have it *good.* "Holy shit, I Am! Holy shit! That bus, that bus, you didn't see—it almost hit me!" I flailed my arms in the direction the bus had bolted, then ran toward him with the intention to pummel him for allowing this to happen. "You *knew* I didn't want to ride a bike in India! This is why! *This is why!* I was almost *killed* and you . . ."

He reached out to grab my arms in futility.

"Fuck, you, fuck you! Get. Get. Get away from me!" From thereon I screeched unintelligibly. My throat felt like it was tearing open. As I looked around, I noticed people staring and gathering to watch our *Jerry Springer* drama of "almost" domestic violence on the streets of India.

"Penelope! Penelope!" Nick said looking into my eyes. "Who is angry? Who is feeling this?"

"Oh, no you don't!" I lashed at him. "No. You. Don't . . . . Let. Me. Go!"

I broke free of his bear hug and spun around ninja-style. I thought about picking up the bike to escape, but . . . *buses. Big. Brown. Buses. Everywhere!*

"Okay, but are you inquiring?" he said loudly enough for the world to hear, or at least the nearest twenty people.

"Of course I am not in-quiring!" I snapped.

"Please, would you," he said with compassion and an authority I could not deny.

Throwing my arms down to my sides, I whirled in a circle as I screamed, "Who. The. *Fuck. Am. IIIIIIII?*"

When I stopped, but not before almost tripping over my loosely Velcroed Tevas, he started laughing. "I don't think that's the Self-inquiry."

That pissed me off even more. But I knew. He was right.

In the midst of such intense fear, anger, and hysteria, time stops—the moment before it all comes clear. One look at his smile and I recognized the shenanigans I was up to. *I've been caught. Cornered. On a wide-open road! In front of a hundred strangers who are not taking my side! Dammit!*

Maybe the anger was grace but I couldn't tolerate the calm on Nick's face. How was he not worried in the slightest that I'd almost been flattened into a human *paratha* (Indian pancake) just moments earlier? I couldn't look at him. I couldn't look at anyone. So I turned inward. And I became fully aware of the rage. I sensed its shape and where it seemed to be in my body. It felt like a knife jutting up from the pit of my stomach, piercing my heart, coming out through my throat. As I looked at it, I became aware that I was aware of it, that this emotion wasn't me, and I wasn't this "I" who was aware of the rage.

Could I accept that rage was present?

Yes.

Could I accept that I could accept it?

Yes.

Now who is aware of this?

I am.

I felt my sense of being expand to contain the whole scene. "Who am I?" I eked out as tears welled behind my still-closed eyes. "Who. Am. I?"

After a long moment, I felt Nick's arm slide around my shoulder again. As he pulled me chest to chest, heart to heart, he kissed my forehead. Our show was over, and although it wasn't quite the time for *Sex in the City* (definitely not on the streets of India), I could at least handle a rerun of *Friends*.

"One more thing, Penelope," Nick whispered in words meant for my ears only. "Who do you think is driving that bus?"

That question hit me much harder than any bus ever could have. My mind stopped and what I realized is that I was never in any danger—not then, not ever.

It had all been in my mind.

The path to this insight was no picnic. Whenever it came time to acknowledge the illusory nature of my dramas, my gut churned in visceral detox. I threw up often, wherever I happened to be, including once on the steps of an Indian café, where dear people brought out brooms and buckets to clean up my mess and Nick gently toweled vomit off my face with a wandering swami's handkerchief. He was my spiritual teacher, yes, but he might not always be there physically when I was tossing my cookies. *I had to face my fears—of people not liking me, of people wanting to hurt me, of buses inadvertently ending me—without clinging to external support.* Learning to fully experience my emotions while turned inward imbued me with the courage to face emotions whenever and wherever they presented themselves from then on.

In time, it was no longer necessary to do my introspective work with Nick around, because it was I who had to accept the circumstances of life. No matter where I went, I could not escape my teacher—even if I called *it* my husband, lover, or my friend—because I could not escape myself.

In All Honesty

A ’70s child on Long Island, I grew up high on Billy Joel, fantasizing *fawh the lawngest* time about one day becoming the uptown girl he’d be singing about. At bedtime, my mother told me tales of having been a groupie of sorts, she and her Catholic high school girlfriends ogling over him during private performances in his garage before he became a musical god among men. With reverence for Billy in her voice, how could I do anything but accept his lyrics as gospel?

One weekend in the early ’80s after Sunday school, I lay sprawled across my frilly, peaches and cream-colored bedspread, listening to music, brooding over my upcoming First Confession. *What sins will I tell the priest I’ve committed? I have to make some up.* I’d been triggered by my portable red tape deck blasting “Honesty.” *Why* was it such a lonely word? It worried me. The fear of alienation burrowed deep in my soul.

During those elementary years, it was the foreboding combination of my mother’s prayer hands and the gleam of my father’s belt buckle that first exposed me to the adage “honesty is the best policy.” This I learned from the few times I’d tested the limits on stretching the truth. I internalized the lesson that it’s important to be honest, not because it always feels good to be truthful, but because through lying I might escape pain. Consequently, this childhood fear delayed my discovery of how liberating it feels to be honest with people, no matter how much the truth might sting.

In adulthood, spiritual practice has taught me that even the sting of "resistance to what is" is not a permanent state but a time-bound emotional response. And when we investigate, *who or what resists?*, it always passes. Yet, if as children we faced punishment for some innocent action and our honest explanation would have yielded a beating but a lie would spare us a spanking, then why not lie? Perhaps it is fated in this world that our guardians taught us to lie, so we could sense the pain of separation and later come to know the joy of reunion.

In the earliest days of *sadhana*, I recognized how "learned lying" was unconsciously carried forward into virtually every area of my life. Yet in no other place did this root pattern resurface so fiercely for review as within my intimate relationship with Nick. There was no skipping over it. I had to look the liar in the heart, understand its fear, honor it for being the shadow whereby I came to know the shining truth, and then decide if I still wished to live the lie or boldly abide in truth.

My internal truth detector that went off when I was lying or being lied to seemed to have been dulled from overexposure to computers, media and society's all-pervasive stimuli, as well as the habit of trusting in others' voices more than in my own. But the moment I committed to live from the truth, my heart opened and this precious sensitivity was revived.

The first time I found myself consciously speaking the truth in a situation where I otherwise would have lied was at work. My boss knocked on my door and held up a bright-blue-jacketed handbook on happiness that had just rolled off the press. As he slid the hardcover across my desk, he said, "I'd like your honest opinion."

As I leafed through the pages, the first thing I noticed in the Table of Contents was that the author had presented the pursuit of happiness as an elusive "quest." The Introduction contained a Zen parable that spoke of a man of wisdom and monks of the highest order. Line one of Chapter One was: "We are questing beasts." Next it offered some examples of things people search for that they believe will bring happiness: Tiger Woods' golf swing, a Boflex-granted set of washboard abs, and a wrinkle-free forehead courtesy of Botox. As I turned back to the Table of Contents to see if there were any relatable chapter titles, keywords jumped off the page, as they do when I speed-read. I spied another reference to the "Questing Beast" alongside "The Tense Young Man Who Didn't Know That He Already Knew" and "The Outward Journey." Nothing about it appealed to me.

Without reading further, I set the book down between us and looked him in the eye. "It is very well done but I don't think it will appeal to women." *Whoa! Where did that come from?* I thought as my pulse spiked above my target heart rate. Half of me was trembling, the other half, confident.

His head cocked as he grimaced.

"You know I respect the author," I said. "Of course it is my opinion but I don't think this language or the examples are going to resonate with the majority of the market."

Did I just say that out loud? Apparently I had.

I don't remember if the boss said anything as he exited my office. I was in too much shock that I had just spoken words he didn't want to hear. I'd later learn by reading the Acknowledgments that my boss had played a significant role in the content development, so much that the author referred to it as "their project." *Oopsie.* I still hear an echo of nails on a chalkboard when considering that, had I been aware of this fact beforehand, I might have praised the book and delayed my fate. Unsettling as it was, I celebrate that moment as major milestone when I, upon being asked for my honest opinion, gave it—no more, no less.

During those *final weeks* inside corporate America, I hit bottom. I did not reach this low point as a result of being substance-addicted, but I was sick. Sick of lies. Sick of office gossip and especially sick of the lies I told—*I'm happy, I'm fine, I don't mind working late*—just so people would like me and so I might believe myself. As my sensitivity increased, I noticed how crappy it felt to lie and to be in the presence of lies and conversations about people when they weren't around. It made my gut wrench, my spine tighten, my nerves burn, and my limbs shake.

So I then began to distance myself from people, social groups, and institutions that tolerated lying. Shortly thereafter, I noticed the dynamics of all my relationships shifting as divine grace presented me opportunities to be honest in areas I previously had not been. Inside and outside of the workplace, I attracted clear-cut opportunities to be honest and vulnerable like never before. What happened one night, after probably my tenth date with Nick, stands out as a prime opportunity I received to be honest . . . in the bedroom.

Nick and I had been in a loving, monogamous relationship for several months by this point, yet secretly I was still experiencing attraction to other men and the desire to be looked at by them. Nick asked me about this immediately after he watched me bat eyelashes at a long-haired, twenty-something hunk who had made eye contact with me in the foyer of the West Palm Beach Cheesecake Factory. And can I just tell you? I denied it throughout dinner and we stayed up all night, lights on in the bedroom, Nick in the armchair and me sitting up on the edge of our bed, as I continued to lie. Of course, my intention was to spare his feelings, as well as eliminate the risk of him ever leaving me; but as I'd later learn he really didn't care about the guy, only that I was lying.

Finally at about 4:00 a.m., I surrendered. "Okay, I flirted with the guy. Are you fucking happy?"

To my surprise he responded, "Yes."

Well, it was as if a vacuum had switched on. Suddenly, all of the tension in the room vanished. Sitting quietly as I watched the emotions empty from my mind for more than an hour, we reached a new depth of intimacy. Around 6:00 a.m., as faint sunbeams streamed through the blinds we never closed, we fell asleep in each other's arms. This was the critical moment when I realized that if either one of us ever wanted to be with someone else, we could. There was nothing to stop us other than ourselves! It was our expressed intention to always tell the truth that supported our commitment to this intimacy that we both valued. The taboo of attraction to others would only pose an issue if I lied about it or otherwise allowed my thoughts to give it a power it didn't have.

Swoosh! My anxiety disappeared. I mean, just like that.

To this day, I recall that sacred night with reverence for truth. One moment of utter honesty, even with so much on the line, released me from a lifetime of lies. My fear of honesty, born in childhood, had just dissolved between the sheets I shared with my husband.

Honesty, to my delight, was no longer a lonely word.

HOLY ANNIVERSARY

 $\mathcal{S}$ ix months after our 2004 trip to India, our first "wedding" anniversary rolled around. Outside of penning Nick a love letter and slipping it onto his meditation chair during the night, I didn't mention it. He was not one to acknowledge birthdays or anniversaries at the time, so I didn't get my hopes up to receive even a card in return. In my heart, I agreed with him that all of life was The Celebration, and that festivities should not be determined by dates on a calendar. Which meant I was stunned to tears when he suggested I pack for the islands. He had booked us a Caribbean cruise!

Aboard the ship, I gazed out the porthole alongside our table for two as the intoxicating aroma of a gourmet filet of sole wafted upward from my plate. The turquoise sea reflected every perceptible shade of blue and green against the sky of a million light rays cast off by the setting sun. Live classical piano music filled the dining room and under our table Nick's hand rested softly on my thigh.

Snuggling into him, I whispered, "This must be heaven."

Just then, a most unwelcome dinner guest joined us.

Take a guess?

Yep, my mind.

All day, I'd been struggling to not ruin our anniversary cruise. Even amidst all this brilliance, complete with a loving partner to share it with, I kept being interrupted by a barrage of "horrible" thoughts. *I've had enough. I've lived in Florida for almost twenty years! How many sunsets and seafood platters can I get excited about? I mean, I love Nick and I'm so grateful he took me here, but seriously how much longer will I have to fake having fun?*

I'm not sure exactly how long this thought-storm rained down, but it seemed like forever, until by providence, before my thoughts totally consumed me, something struck me as fishy and caused another pause in the mind stream. For a brief moment, I set down my silverware and paused. My breathing slowed to a stop and I felt peacefully caught in the gaze of the ocean, the sky, and the stars.

Once my breath returned to normal, the sensation of being held by the universe dissipated and I became aware of my body again. I leaned my chin onto my folded hands and said to Nick, "All this beauty *could* get old after a while, unless you remember it's all in you." His brown eyes and tan face beamed and we connected in silence until I made one request. "If I ever act like I've forgotten the beauty, will you please remind me of this moment?"

He nodded.

Anniversary sex—especially when it commences on a cruise ship balcony where deep kisses distract you from the wind about to blow your silky bathrobe out to sea—should be romantic. Leave it to me, though, to be weighted down by an OCD parade of past lovers, right in the heat of the action.

If OMG had been a common expression back then, I might have blurted it out, but my frown said it all.

Nick paused and asked in a whisper, "What's on your mind?"

"Nothing . . . I'm meditating," I said, desperate to convince myself I wasn't thinking. With sabotaging visuals of other men flashing across my mental screen, I could not have possibly felt more separate from the otherwise perfect, breathtaking moment I'd dreamed of all my life.

"Let's meditate," he said.

In hindsight, *that* made it more perfect, didn't it?

Yet at the time, I resented the ixnay on our steady climb toward orgasm. But even worse, I felt terrified to admit the untamable lust in my imagination. How could I ever explain all the men in the naked conga line, one of which was South Park's own Eric Cartman? Now do you get where this is going?

We entered the cabin and sat down to meditate. As I practiced being still, Nick's question tickled my inner ear. "Is there anything you would like to communicate with me?"

He was not prying; it was not like that at all. It was him understanding and honoring who I was. With Catholic conditioning, I could only let loose in the wake of confession and repentance. *But how could he not judge me for this?* I agonized and trembled over it. Then it just blurted out, the most shameful secret I'd ever tried to bury inside.

"I just had the thought of another man's penis!" I said and started to cry. "And another, and another, and I'm sorry, I'm so sorry."

Nick smiled. "And who just had the thought?"

"What?" I said, "Oh, I did."

Nick didn't look upset. In fact, his eyes drank me in more than ever.

"Remember your insight today? That All is inside You."

He hadn't meant to mix metaphors, but the mind didn't squander the pun handed to it on a silver freakin' platter. The thought of another naked man inside me proved too much. I'd never known my inner capacity for this level of meltdown . . . which is left best undescribed.

Until suddenly I asked myself, "Who is thinking this?"

I am.

Now, *who am I?*

Feeling calmer, almost peaceful, I had one more question that I was both scared to ask and too afraid not to. So, I spouted, "What if this craziness happens again?"

Nick asked, "Who cares?"

Puzzled by his nonresistance, I followed up. "How do you know this was not reflecting a subconscious desire to be back with my exes?"

Again, Nick shot a look that catapulted my attention to the depths of my heart.

"Because I know Who You Are," he said, kissing my forehead. "And here you are, right now."

I Do

Sunlight on the ocean dances

a thousand diamonds

for all the ways

this romance is

ten thousand reminders

of infinite chances

at deep listening,

eyes glistening

as you hear

yourself say

Yes, I do

to Love

today

STRIPPING AWAY THE WHORE COMPLEX

*C*uddled in Nick's arms in the ashram commons area, I meditated while we waited for the other residents to be seated for a spontaneous movie night. One of the guys ran his finger down our stack of conscious films and stopped on a DVD case I didn't recognize. An impromptu gathering around a randomly selected movie was my favorite way to watch one. It was akin to opening up a book to any page and then reading it—the outer message would always be a reflection of what was going on within.

Though I'd never seen it before, *Spring, Summer, Fall, Winter . . . and Spring* felt instantly familiar. A novice Buddhist monk goes to live with a master in a peculiar monastery, a floating dock upon a lake within a virgin forest. The story depicts the evolution of the master-disciple relationship over the course of the boy's youth into his adulthood. In a culminating act of self-discipline, the disciple ties a hefty grinding stone to his body, collects a Buddha statue in his hands, and embarks on a symbolic trek up a wooded mountainside. Upon reaching the summit, he prays and leaves behind the stone, with the Buddha statue on top.

Once the closing credits rolled to a stop, the screen went black along with the whole room . . . and that's when Nick asked, "What is your stone?"

The silence was tangible as someone flicked on the lights. We all looked around at one another, squirming deeper into our seats to escape our teacher's gaze. I watched my thoughts line up into military-style formation as my mind defended my gut answer. Suddenly, everyone conveniently drifted away, leaving only myself and one of the men. Nick drew our attention to the fact that most will not complete this journey in this lifetime.

This man's answer hinged on his physical appearance, his bulging muscles symbolic of the weight of measuring up to the idealized image of a man. As he spoke, I recalled the opening scene of a different movie, *Adaptation*, where Nicholas Cage's character, Donald Kaufman, wrestles with the same despair. Donald internally debates whether he should get his hair cut short to mask his baldness. He tells himself to be "real" and "confident" as he struggles with the pressure on men to look desirable.

Wow. My friend was a gorgeous man, still is. It was the first time I ever deeply considered that a guy could feel this way. I'd been too busy shaving my legs, painting my face, and climbing to nowhere on my Stairmaster, to even consider that the men I was chasing might be similarly drenched in the sweat of self-doubt, also running on a treadmill. Yet, I came to learn as he set down his stone that it hung deeper. The root, the final fig leaf, was penis-size insecurity. Would his member be long and thick enough to satisfy a woman and thus, by the mind's logic, be loved by her?

"Penelope?" Nick whispered.

Uh oh, my turn.

But my friend's valiant honesty inspired me to just blurt it out. "Okay, I'm afraid people think I'm a whore."

Then I crossed my legs, as if that would change anything.

It wouldn't. It was over. I'd said it. And surprisingly, no scarlet "A" appeared on my chest. These guys didn't even flinch! They just sat there listening.

Next I purged the story of how, at my first wedding, I overheard my father bragging to some guests that I was still a virgin. Of course it wasn't true, yet I was glad to hear him sounding so sure of it and hoped they would believe it, too. It was my last-ditch opportunity to be seen as pure as Mary . . . and my father, of all people, was hooking me up. That is, until he got drunk and started grinding on me on the dance floor. I was tipsy and too busy making sure no red wine spilled on my gown to even question his bawdy behavior, much less stand up to him and demand that he stop, an option which didn't occur to me either. I laughed away the tears forming on the ledges of my eyes. "Have you ever heard anything so ridiculous?!"

"Is there anything else beneath that laugher?" Nick probed.

Hail Mary. There is. Am I really going to say th . . .

"Yes, I'm scared to look directly at a penis—and I'm afraid that means I want to."

How apropos. Here is a guy concerned that his organ didn't measure up . . . and there I was, a gal too frightened to even look at one.

It was true. I was terrified of the penis. One weekend morning when I was a child, I walked in on my father in the bathroom, where he was taking a shower. I had come from the kitchen on a mission to find out if he wanted ham or bologna on his lunch sandwich. (*Interesting coinkydink, eh?*) When he pulled back the curtain and inadvertently exposed himself to me, "Dammit, I thought you were your mother!" were not his only words. He berated me to a degree that I could never again eat bologna (which he did order at the end of his tirade) without feeling sick, or curious about what I had gotten into so much hot water for laying my eyes on.

The men remained still. No one scolded me or asked me to leave the room. Fear lost its chokehold—I felt heard. I felt seen. It was liberating to cry as I laid my soul bare with these dear friends as my witness. The level of intimacy in this conversation was against my religion and everything conditioned into me since fourth grade, when the boys were separated from the girls to watch "The Film" about our respective genitalia and I was informed that "good girls don't talk about private parts with boys." Two decades later, it was done. This man and I had been true and revealed to each other our "worst"—and I had a new lease on what it meant to be good.

As I meditated, my stone fell to the floor.

LOVING THE WHOLE PACKAGE

*A*t age thirty-one, I found myself stripped of the posh South Florida lifestyle, which I exchanged for cabin life in a Costa Rican mountain river valley along the *Cerro de la Muerte*. The crisp air that streamed in beneath the hand-carved front door kept me alert in meditation until the late hours. Once Nick had fallen into *samadhi** beneath woven blankets, I would deepen in my eyes-open practice by knitting warm scarves in colorful patterns resembling birds of the cloud forest. My cozy Buddha chair was set beside an iMac with a trusty dial-up Internet connection, which allowed me the dual pleasure of researching avian anatomy to inspire my handicraft and staying intermittently in touch with the world.

One night, I googled for red, green, and teal eyelash yarn to mimic the feathers of the resplendent quetzal, a thirteen-inch bird and our closest neighbor in the wilderness. My search led me to *Crazy Aunt Purl*, a popular knitter's blog, where I randomly clicked on "Contact Us." What popped up? A photo of a sexy librarian-type woman whose thought bubble said, "That postman has a large package . . . "

---

* Meditative absorption in the bliss of Being.

A surge of laughter welled in my belly before it escaped my lips. Nick's head cocked slightly. I giggled once more before he whispered, "What's so funny?"

I reached with both arms to turn the monitor toward him.

"Ladies who knit, you've gotta love us!" I squeaked.

"What's even funnier is that *you* are looking at that website," he replied through a soft grin before closing his eyes and returning to the bliss.

That's when it hit me.

There I was, living all Walden Pond-style in a gingerbread house in a remote forest of Central America, and my most re-sisted thoughts of the male genitalia had *found me* out here in the middle of nowhere. Other instances had brought this *vasana** to my attention, but Nick's closing his eyes and returning to NowHereLand was my cue from the Universe that I had to face this resistance on my own.

I reflected on Nick's observation, acknowledging its pene-trating truth. I didn't have to lift a single page in my library of spiritual books to find the magic clue I most needed to awaken. A website graphic perfectly mirrored the fact that I was still obsessed with the penis—and I was ready to face the shame I felt about that. As easily as I could have brushed it off by telling myself, "Well, that is someone else's website and so that's about her and not me," that would have been a big, fat lie. Because I knew in my heart that everything I encountered was about me, exposing the shape of my own mind. How else could I be seeing it or attracting it into my experience? Why else would I be giggling at a penis joke on the screen of my computer—er, the screen of my awareness? I obviously had not yet resolved my inner conflict about the male sex organ.

---

* Sanskrit term for an often unconscious, karmic tendency or pattern that is said to incite rebirth. It is similar to *sin* in the Judeo-Christian tradition.

First, I searched the mental archives of my grad school research papers. *Maybe there was something to Freud's theory of penis envy. Maybe I feared the penis because I desired one, and maybe I desired a penis so as to know it was nothing to be afraid of.* Logical as it seemed, this thought really didn't calm me, so I looked deeper.

Was I the only woman who could not tell you whether the men I was once with were circumcised? I admit it. Ever since the shower incident with my father, I never looked directly at penises. It seemed strange to me that I harbored such a deep fear of even sneaking a peek down there. Suddenly, that uncomfortable feeling turned into sadness. I was sure my former therapist would have considered this a good topic for our sessions, had I then had any consciousness whatsoever of this complete mental block.

As I started to feel emotions surfacing, I touched the roots of this sadness, tracing it further back than the shower scene to the childhood innocence of happily bathing with my younger brother one day, and the very next being told that it was time for us to take separate baths. Of course, in the case of siblings, this would seem like sound parenting. Yet the way this information got stored in my mental database was that it applied to men across the board. It was never reprogrammed with an "it's okay, wonderful even, to share in the sensory experience of your lover's manhood."

Being a child who listened dutifully to my mother, I didn't think much about this change after it had taken place: I had so many other important things to do while my brother was taking his bath, like finishing my homework and straightening the furniture in my Barbie DreamHouse. At the time, it didn't seem that anything profound had occurred. Yet, in fact, a cornerstone of my conditioning had been laid: my genitalia was mine, a boy's or man's was his, and peeking was forbidden! My father's screaming response to my accidental sighting of his penis painfully reinforced this rule.

This exploration helped to unravel complex emotions of sadness and guilt that I'd felt, in one way or another, almost every day of my life. As a young competitive swimmer, I saw boys in Speedos on most afternoons throughout my middle school years. Dodging my eyes from bulging penises nearly made me cross-eyed. Upon later becoming highly concerned with my schoolwork and pleasing male coaches with my athletic excellence in the pool, I didn't have time to think about penises . . . I mean boys. So why look anyway? Not to mention, I was nearsighted and these were the days before cheap contact lenses; so from behind my cap and goggles, I could only clearly see what was about three or four feet in front of me . . . that is, without squinting. Which was a good thing, because what if my parents had caught me peeping on the walk to the locker room after practice? What kind of trouble could *that* have meant for Miss Goody Two Fins?

Next, I re-experienced the shame that reared its head (no pun intended) in eighth grade, when I'd finally landed a boyfriend. Or at least there was this boy who met me once at the cinema after my mother dropped me off at the mall. I could probably tell you the name of every movie I've ever been to and with whom, except for this one. Because my only memory of that day—other than sharing a Swensons hot fudge sundae before the movie—is a three-dimensional, multisensory montage of dimly lit blackness, an overdose of Drakkar Noir, and a young man's sweaty palm reaching in slow motion to hold mine, lifting it and placing it— yep, you got it—right on his package. I didn't know why it felt like a rock to the touch and imagined it must have been the texture of his black, acid-washed jeans. Or perhaps it was a large zipper? Z. Cavariccis were all the rage then, so maybe what I felt was just a new style of pants? I honestly had been kept in the dark about how the penis hardened with arousal. *Arousal* wasn't even in my vocab yet. All I felt was that my hand did not belong there, and so not a moment later, I whispered four and a half words I regretted the rest of my eighth-grade life.

"Uh, no thanks . . . that's yours."

After years of meditation, spiritual practice, and not minding what other people say, I barely remembered the feeling of embarrassment. But when I recalled the incident, and how I earned the nickname "That's Yours" by all the cool kids, I merged with the heartbreak and disgrace that arose when they'd chanted this phrase as I carried my lunch tray through their territory in the cafeteria. As ashamed as I'd felt though, I was also thrilled that they were paying me attention, so the trauma seemed worth it. And even though my family moved across town after graduation and I never had to face these particular boys again, in my mind I was still running from them, yet craving their attention all the while. A fear and desire so energized, it got transferred onto every man in my presence, every day possible minute.

And these confusing emotions were not things I could have talked about with my stress counselors. I was too afraid they would think I was a tart for being curious about men's bodies, much less wanting men to look at mine. So, I hadn't ever considered the emotions intertwined in this dynamic with any level of awareness until that night in the cabin, when the story unwound with the inquiry, "To whom did all of this drama occur?"

Awash in the peace of Self-inquiry, I put away my yarn and needles for the night. An odd, pointy thread of my personal story had been unraveled, and deep in meditation I was again naked of the desire to collect any more threads, let alone knots.

The fresh air in the cabin was still cold, but the evanescent joy of releasing this lifelong drama into the ether heated my body like a furnace. I turned off the light, crawled under our pile of blankets, and snuggled up to Nick feeling indescribably light, free, and . . . well, a little bit frisky!

PART FOUR

Secrets of the Blessed Marriage

A Carriage and Two Doves

I love marriage

I love its glories

I love its transcended war stories

I love how Love lets neither lover

cling nor run for cover

I love how Love sets neither one above the other

I love how marriage and Love

go together like a carriage

and two doves —

wild and free to fly

yet choosing to ride

side by side

FAIL-SAFE COMPATIBILITY TEST

*H*ow can I know for sure if my lover and I are compatible? This question frequently woke me up at night in the weeks leading up to my divorce. During the daytime, I met the anxiety by locking myself in the bedroom and practicing beginner yoga on DVD. My then-husband and I had started taking a yoga class at the gym, but it brought up so many feelings that ever since I farted during a shoulder stand and he cracked up, causing a minor scene, I desperately needed privacy. My solo classes at home ended when the sobbing started. To hide evidence of my despair, I wiped my tears and hid the red blotches under my eyes with cover-up before joining my husband for dinner. It went on like this until one afternoon when I could barely lift myself off the mat. I lingered in corpse pose, licked a tear off my lip, and prayed aloud for a true spiritual teacher to guide me out of this facade of a marriage.

"I need a spiritual teacher," I said. "Please! *I need a real spiritual teacher.* It doesn't have to be anyone famous, just someone who understands what I am going through and can show me the way to real love. Thank you. Amen."

This prayer that escaped my lips felt like the only thing I could hold on to. My marriage wasn't working, despite all of the counseling. The romantic dinners prepared. The expensive outfits purchased to resemble the women of the country club. The German lessons and heart-to-heart conversations attempted in each other's native tongues. The golf lessons I took in a final attempt to salvage the relationship. If you were to watch *Love Actually* in reverse, that backward movement was us. My every effort to connect took me further from the connection I had once felt. There was nothing else I could do to change the feeling that I was no longer what he wanted. And I could not deny the longing in my heart—I was still a seeker, not yet a finder of love. Apparently being well-matched had nothing to do with things of the world. The smack of the judge's gavel at my divorce hearing woke me up to the fact that I had no clue what compatibility actually meant.

When Nick and I fell in love, I became obsessed with cracking the compatibility code. The need to know we'd make it was the "boomerang effect" to my newfound meditation practice where not knowing was The Way. When I asked him if he thought we were compatible, he whispered a Forrest Gump impression in my ear, the line about going together like peas and carrots. I giggled so hard I ever so slightly peed my pants. That is the moment I proposed turning our relationship into a scientific case study on compatibility. He loved the idea too, and so we engaged in regular conversations on the subject.

Answers to the compatibility conundrum did not come quickly, but they were well worth the hours of contemplation. We not only observed our own daily habits, but those of couples who spent time with us in Tantra sessions. While teaching the art of conscious communication and relationship, we collected data to answer our research questions:

- *What do all of the compatible couples have in common?*

- *Are there traceable reasons people find themselves flipping the relationship-status button on and off with the frequency of a strobe light?*

- *Is it really that complicated?*

For the record, this study was not scientific. We approached the experiment qualitatively through observation of stories. For example, we didn't consider whether the partners had ever been married before or the amount of time each person had been single prior to entering into the relationship. In the end, matters of time hold no meaning in the timeless dimension of love. Thus Nick and I agreed that such factors had little, if any, significance.

Most people assume physical attraction is nonnegotiable in a successful relationship, yet we found that someone's degree of attraction to their lover's body held no sway over their ability to remain happily coupled. Confusion about physical attraction often complicates matters for couples; we observed that, contrary to what society teaches people to believe, not everybody feels attracted to their lover 100 percent of the time. In our eyes, physical desire is just a pawn anyway, one that keeps lovers in the game long enough to recognize the reflection of inner beauty that is the actual magnetism all along. Also, the degree of physical attraction appeared to support relationships as much as it seemed to confuse them, so we ruled it out as a fail-safe compatibility factor.

Many people base their compatibility on whether they argue or fight. Although it may be indicative, I knew through hindsight into my first marriage that this factor is not definitive. My ex and I almost never argued, a fact in which I took great pride. Actually,

I clung to it for my sense of security, so much that I almost always stopped myself from expressing how I truly felt just to dodge an argument. Whenever I share this with someone in conversation, I get an "amen!" because repression has been a common experience . . . and in our heart of hearts we know that this behavior, by smothering truth, suffocates love.

Now just because incompatible couples don't argue very often is not to say that the opposite is true and that compatible couples argue all the time—certainly not! A compatible couple's relationship is held together by some deeper, intangible glue that is strong enough to withstand any argument, so they do not avoid disagreement. For lovers committed to acceptance and thus, spiritual awakening, the passing storm of a disagreement is usually a sign of our own "need to be right," which our partner is simply mirroring back to us. Through arguments with Nick, I learned that I did not need to *do* anything about this conditioned pattern; indeed, I could not change it if I tried. Awareness of it—and acceptance of the fact that I once believed in the importance of being right—led me to understand the profound implications of my soul's answer to the proverbial question, "Would you rather be right, or would you rather be happy?"

It's true, I used to run from a lover's quarrel faster than a nerd escaping the gym during dodgeball (also me). But I have actually come to enjoy a spontaneous spat with Nick. It always ends in laughter where I win the bonus prize: identifying the position I'm holding on to that is preventing my happiness. Where fail-safe compatibility was concerned, Nick and I never argued about the three factors that we found most accurately indicate a couple's intimate relativity. Whether these resonate with you or shock you to the core, they are significant in bringing human perception beyond the visual attraction most people rely on above their more subtle and primal instincts.

The first is (drum roll, please): musical tastes.

What? Get outta here!

Nope, sorry if this irritates you. The music someone enjoys reflects the vibrational relativity of their mind, which molds one's physical environment and shapes their universe. On this metaphysical level, music transcends perceivable dimensions as well. For instance, while I was decimating my parents' Bee Gees album on a pink plastic record player in my childhood home on Long Island, Nick was tearing up the disco floors to "Stayin' Alive" in South Florida. Despite apparent variance in time and space, our musical appetites bordered on identical when we met two decades later, even with Nick thirteen years older than me. That's the power of vibration. Of course, it is not an exact science as certainly no two lovers agree on every single song, yet we have found "What are your top-five favorite songs?" to be an ideal first-date question. You won't want to underestimate the significance of this one!

Music is such a powerful transmitter of energy, it can transform an environment into heaven or hell. In fact, we've tested this too. If you want an aggressive person to leave your physical space, you can influence this ever so subtly by turning on a peaceful melody. Its ethereal qualities will sufficiently transform the space to where the belligerent person (who ultimately turns out to be an outpicturing of your mind) will suddenly have to leave or be drawn away by some seemingly "unrelated" incident. Maybe their cell phone rings or nature calls, only you'll know their departure wasn't an accident. On the flip side, this principle can be used to "set the tone" for harmonious interaction and to create healing spaces as well.

Compatibility factor number two has been mastered by the largest and smallest, furriest and fuzziest animals all over the planet. Have you guessed it yet? Yep, body scent...or should I say *booty* scent? Either way, the fragrance of the body is so essential in determining relativity that a dog can know in seconds what takes humans hours, months, even years or a lifetime to figure out. Who knew? Our good olfactory glands can pre-relieve us of many painful years of relationship distress. As Nick and I have often joked, why torture yourself needlessly when such simple wisdom lies right under your nose?

The creators of pheromone parties have figured this out. Having not attended such a party, I cannot personally attest to the effectiveness, but the idea of scent-based matchmaking events makes perfect sense! Pheromones are airborne biochemical molecules released into the environment by our bodies; research has proven that their scent is a unique expression of our moods, our sexual orientation, and even our genetics. Yet isn't it intriguing that neither a single scientist nor whole teams of them funded by the world's leading perfume manufacturers have been able to isolate and duplicate these primal chemical cues? And thank goodness! Could you imagine the mass chaos if tens of thousands of people who were nothing alike were able to manipulate their scents to smell attractive to one another?

It's no secret: Nick smells incredibly good to me, and I to him—well, maybe not during a detox diet but definitely at all other times. Yes, even after a good workout. He and I experienced a blessed and fast beginning to our intimate relationship, so it did not take long to figure this out. For anyone approaching a relationship at a more gradual rate, you might kiss their hand as part of your greeting as you sneak a quick whiff of it, assuming it is socially awkward to hug them instantly when you first meet. Though you may risk looking like a pervert if caught, the old hug 'n' sniff is, of course, the most effective way to see if you dig someone's body scent. If you don't like it, the person may still make a wonderful friend, yet they will probably not be a compatible lover. Try it and see for yourself, or reflect on personal experiences with your current partner or past lovers as they pertain to this keystone of compatibility.

Before you put that sniffer to work though, I must divulge one other pheromone-related thing. It's something that I did not want to admit at first, especially the time I came home from work on the day of "Hurricane I Am" to find Nick had lined up all of the bottles of Chanel No. 5, Opium, and dozens of my hoarded perfume samples on the edge of the kitchen sink. I had to remind myself that I signed up for this type of surprise when I told him I'd choose for him to be a teacher before a husband; now he had been thoughtful enough to empower me with the option of pouring every ounce of perfume I'd spent hard-earned money on, and precious hours collecting, down the drain. "If you are hiding how you really smell, what else are you hiding?" were his exact words.

This stunk—literally. It felt painful to look so deeply, and yet it was worth every insight, as this questioning, combined with Self-inquiry, peeled back the layers of the proverbial onion. Pouring out my perfume was just the beginning; until I learned to accept and even enjoy my own body scent, I remained abusive to my body in thought, self-talk, and deed, constantly thinking *I need it to look different too: thinner, curvier, more toned.* This is not to say that throwing out perfume is the panacea to a distorted self-image, but it definitely helped me pinpoint other areas of suffering on account of body identification. Based on Nick's full disclosure of his aromas, I drew the generalized conclusion that when someone does nothing to hide their natural scent, they're also quite likely to love you "Just the Way You Are." (Yes, when we met, that Billy Joel song was on both our iPods.)

My heart blossomed in response to this insight. I had come to know my Self to be that same space (for lack of a better word) of unconditional acceptance. No longer was I bound to an image of myself as a flawed human, ruled by unconscious programming that insists I should be something other than exactly what I am. *This that accepts everything, this that loves, this that I am is not even a physical thing!*

Compatibility shares the same roots as *compassion*, where *com-* means "with, together" and *pati-* "to suffer." Good thing it had not occurred to me to extract meaning from root words until later in the experiment, because at one point I might have defined compatibility as the ability to suffer alongside a partner in a relationship, each miserable in our own ways, rather than understanding the deeper significance of what it means to *suffer with* someone. What it really means is to put myself in their shoes, for the purposes of not only understanding their pain but also realizing that, given their precise set of past mental conditioning and circumstances, I would have acted and suffered in exactly the same way. All leading to the revelation that they could not have done "it" differently because "their" thoughts are arising from the exact same Source as "mine"— and when I know myself to be that Source, is there really any difference between us?

Hence compatibility factor number three—*two lovers' absolute acceptance of each other*—is the only fail-safe compatibility test. *Am I willing to imagine myself in their shoes? Can I accept what I'm resisting about my partner? Do I recognize this as an area in me that I have not been able to accept before seeing it in the perfect mirror that they are? Can I accept that I accept it?* This acceptance process circumvents the physical senses and yet mysteriously seems to remain palpable. With it, what felt like a dense and difficult life takes on the ethereal, flowing quality of a dream. This brand of total acceptance cannot be bought in stores, yet it is all we will ever need.

The Compatibility Prayer

Thank You for gifting me

the readiness

to drop all definitions of

what I was willing to accept as love

so I could remember

the Love

that accepts me

just as I Am

WHEN HIS YANG MET MY YIN

*W*hen I close my eyes, I can still see Mr. Greenstein, my silver-haired, perpetually tanned, seventh-grade science teacher, clanking together two shiny horseshoe magnets before my widened eyes to prove "opposites attract." Mind you, I had a colossal crush on this man. After all, I was a very mature eleven, and he ... well, my grandfather's age. Oh, but he was so extremely wise in the ways of science that I worshipped his wealth of knowledge as simply irrefutable.

Throughout my school days, my mad crushes on science teachers blinded me to the finer truths of life. I never questioned the "facts" they taught me. Until I married Nick, a retired high school science teacher who cajoled me to be still and ponder this:

What if everything you've ever learned was wrong?

Glancing at life on the surface, it appeared that opposites attract. In fact, if you compare my husband's history with mine, they could not possibly have been more opposite. He was brought up an unreservedly loving child in the freewheeling '60s, whereas I was bred a timid kid-in-a-clamshell during the fear-infused '80s. Nick evolved into an All-State soccer stud and collegiate national champion football star who played outdoors all day and almost never studied; and I became a locally acclaimed band nerd who went straight to her bedroom to do homework, pausing only to apply Clearasil, watch *The Golden Girls*, and get 8.5 hours of shut-eye. When we met as adults, Nick's mind was already still as he had been teaching meditation, whereas mine more closely resembled a jumping bean with ADD. As for our overall stats, he enjoyed movies and I preferred books. I'd sought brains in lovers, while he had gravitated toward . . . the more physical attributes. *We were living, breathing proof that opposites attract.*

How could we *not* have spent our frisky first dates bursting with orgasmic laughter while we rubbed up against our polarized predispositions and charmingly opposite perspectives? Just like Mr. Greenstein's magnets, we clicked! Apparently, because we were opposite in almost every way, we instantly became inseparable. Everyone, from our chiropractor to complete strangers, commented on the harmony we radiated together.

I talked virtually incessantly (during dates, dinners, movies, and even sex); he listened endlessly. I roused him; he calmed me. And somewhere between his always running early and my old habit of running late, we wound up in the middle way: right on time—usually.

On one of those old scrambling-to-get-ready days (which still happen occasionally, I admit) I got caught in a mood and quipped, "If time is an illusion, then am I really late?" Now, Nick's a guy who belly laughs at my jokes and will go a lot of philosophical places with me, but he wouldn't tread there.

Instead, we went to the next stage of relationship.

You know what I mean: the one where you realize that your differences, which once seemed "oh so cute," are now grating on your nerves, costing your precious REM sleep, and challenging your sanity. Yet, for me, this was a critical period during which our polar-"opposite" qualities nudged me to look deeper and probe, "What is it about this person that is irritating me so much?" This I wrestled with until finally surrendering to the fact that it is not about the other person at all, but me. Because what I resist in someone else is actually an area in myself I have not yet accepted.

Before I learned to embrace my first husband as my mirror, I had opted for a speedy divorce. In so doing, I lured a whole new series of train wrecks to me, through which I had additional opportunities to find this same mirror staring right back at me, only with different frames. When the mirror effect is acknowledged as true, then couples are poised for Self-realization, the heart's knowing that contrast is merely an appearance and that we are reflections of the same essence.

In other words, it is not opposite charges that pull people together but the universal Law of Attraction: *like energies attract.* Despite scientific explanations on positive and negative energies attracting, magnets stick together because it's their natural design. That's just what magnets do. Nick and I were drawn together like magnets and in our shared space, our resonant thought-vibrations comprised our joint reality. We stood in the same kitchen, slept in the same bed, and drew from the same bank account day after day (and still do). Our home, from my perspective, had become a perfect laboratory for observing how Nick's "less than desirable" behaviors were actually manifestations of the same repressed energies that I wanted to express without inhibition. It used to especially bother me when he slurped his soup, belched, or fell asleep when I was still talking to him at night. What else could I do but notice my conditioned judgements, accept these natural occurrences, and let my prissy defenses dissolve in the light of my desire for ultimate liberation?

Seemingly opposite or not, he and I were magnetized to each other for inimitable reasons, and on this topic I will say no more because sharing such intimate details invites two unwelcome guests: unsolicited advice and her restless cousin, drama. Just that once I stopped pointing my finger at Nick as the source of my problems and frustration, I came to see "his" annoying behaviors as actions steeped in God's grace. It purified my soul—the repeat opportunities to transcend the urge to run away from home at such moments, to feel in my bones the shift from Ohms to OM (resistance to acceptance). All opposites and conflict dissolve in this game of surrender. Our true home is a playground of unbreakable peace wherein I found enough space for his yang and my yin. Where I reside now, there is room for everything.

THE DAY BLAME VANISHED FOREVER

*"You know that when I hate you, it is because I love you
to a point of passion that unhinges my soul."*

—JEANNE JULIE ÉLÉONORE DE LESPINASSE

June 3, 2010

Dear Nick,

*What this woman with the regally long name says is true. I
can no longer keep it inside. I love you so much, part of me
hates you. Because in my love for you, there is nothing left of
me. Within six years of marriage, our lives have merged to a
point where I can barely recognize myself anymore. Before we
met, I was mostly on track to being everything I thought I was
supposed to be. But now? I've lost everything I was taught to
desire. Is it silly to be looking for it in the pages of my journal?*

*I am desperate to find direction again. Will it ever return,
that sense—real or not—that I know where my life is headed?*

It's almost funny now to hear myself say "my life." Is there such a thing? I feel time stripping me of the innocence (perhaps it is ignorance) of believing I have any say in my destiny.

Some people from my past have noticed a change in me and have urged me to leave you. What they do not seem to understand is that I do not try to stay and that I did not try to fall in love with you; I just love you. When I try to not love you, I can't, which shows me that this love is real.

In worldly endeavors, I have not been productive in your absence or presence. Right now, I need time to unwind from the tension of trying to build a life around you when I can't even build one around myself.

My skin tingled with goose bumps as I stared down at the open journal centered in my lap, my legs pretzeled in half-lotus, my hips propped up on a cushion we kept on the condo balcony. We had been living there a month. We'd just moved back to Florida from Costa Rica and for the first time, I was doing exactly what I wanted to do in this spot: meditate, relax, gaze at the ocean, listen to the waves, watch the sunrise, drink my latte ... oh, and write.

For whatever reason, it had taken me thirty sleepless nights to land there. It seemed so simple. *I am ten steps from my bed, so why did it take me so long to arrive?* Suddenly it became clear, all the ways I had pinned the blame on Nick. Insanely, I'd held him responsible for my not spending quiet mornings on the balcony as I wished, despite his frequent reminders that it was always only up to me how I spent my time.

This blame game ended on this day, when I simply woke up, prepared a chai, grabbed pen and paper, stepped outside, and wrote. I couldn't put my finger on exactly where my conditioned pattern to deny following my bliss had come from. I'd learned the behavior to tend to my husband's needs to the exclusion of my own. Until that moment, I thought I would be perceived as unloving if I went off on my own, if only to the balcony for an hour. That is how deeply I had become attached to and afraid of losing him, even in a relationship where both of us were wholeheartedly committed to vigilance over the mind's shenanigans.

In the loving action taken on this day, the cure had revealed itself: simply noticing, with curiosity and non-judgment, these senses of attachment, fear, and obligation, and then following their trail back to the Source. The underlying thought was that if I were to pursue writing, which for me requires periods of aloneness, Nick would be hurt or angry with me. *But this isn't true, because he doesn't care what I do!* As I journaled on, I discovered that my sense of duty toward him was tied to my own fear of being alone. *But who is this "I" that was afraid?*

I saw it! It was the job of the illusory "I" the ego sense, to instill this fear and negative emotion to bar me from the blank page where I hear the still, small voice clearly and know myself as that I Am, my Self, my own teacher. Whenever writing leads me to this inner space overflowing with compassion, love, and joy, all my stories come together ... and fall apart.

To land in this cave where the inner voice echoes and challenges my every belief—at first it felt scary. Yet in showing up *within,* I discovered a new dimension of safety where I am protected from the deadly edges of my own excuses. In this sacred place, I am no longer inclined to use the outer circumstances of my life as a reason for not returning here regularly, to this love-infused presence where I am unlimited, and where all the mistakes I ever made melt into meaninglessness. From here, nothing means anything and so all things are possible.

I had used my relationship as an excuse for not returning here. I also used sex. And food. And money. I casted blame on each of these blessings, in ways that morphed them into curses. Fueled by compulsions to fire another orgasm, to eat more food than necessary, and to earn more and more coin, I developed a love/hate relationship with my partner and all of these things. Sex, food, and money had become my holy trinity. I loved them because I craved them, hated them because I feared I wouldn't always have them—and paradoxically used them as excuses for not consistently turning inward to the one Source with the effortless power to allow me the experience of them all.

The ego sense had twisted it so perfectly, as if into a tightly wound ball of string that, when unraveled, would lead me back to my True Self. Even as I journaled through this luminous wave of insight and love, I battled thoughts of skipping out to eat breakfast, go have sex, or get to my day job instead of writing. I even got up and hit my head on the doorframe, insanely peeking into the bedroom to see if Nick was eating breakfast in bed without me—not that it had ever happened before, but *what if?* My thoughts had launched a desperate hunt for reasons to not return to the blank page. It was a vicious cycle . . . until I spied it. Then came a divine urge stronger than my old habits, softly, gently, and patiently pulling me back outside, like a marionette on a string, to write—to face the blank space where all my excuses would be called out before me and could no longer have an ounce of power over me. Here they could be seen, appreciated, even loved, for the suffering they induced that led me to this climax of blame's great unraveling.

And that is the story of how, on June 3, 2010, blame not only took a back seat to freedom, it vanished forever. Doing what I was born to do—write—led to the space of freedom from *striving* to design a life around "me," not to mention my lover. Right there on the balcony, I decided the only content of my life would be contentment. I committed my heart to writing, content to let my story fall apart.

As Nick lies fast asleep beside me in our bed, the breath of life flowing through his nose in a wispy whistle, I wonder how I could ever blame him for anything when he is not even there . . .

Make-Up Kiss

In a breath, I remember

I Am

All There Is

I even see my name in b l am e —

and smile at how ubiquitous I am

Laughing now,

for never was there ever

a tame make-up kiss.

My, oh my,

could there be a better game

than this?

LOVE LISTENS

*A*s a writer, I am fascinated with language and how its dual purpose is to nurture and provoke through words and the feelings they evoke. I've lost sleep to the mystery of how a single word choice irritates while another soothes. And how, ultimately, the rightness or wrongness of diction is impossible to prove. Language, like a magic wand, can be used to weave understanding or misunderstanding.

Nick and I often wake each other up at twilight to swap reflections on the cosmic ironies that ensue in a media landscape where so many humans have their own handheld printing press. We have shared a chuckle or two about how "communication" is perhaps the most misunderstood word in the English language. In the blaring light of social media, this word "communication" evokes images that the human mind attaches words to using smart phones, laptops, tablets, and other glowing gadgets that more often than not distract it from Self-awareness. When I took up meditation as a daily practice and committed to marriage with my spiritual teacher, it was a relief to set down my cell phone and remember that true communication has nothing to do with a device. That it is a holy communion. Holy because I am one with all of existence, which naturally contains and is contained within the one I am communicating with.

Early on, this knowing inspired me to value all communication opportunities as sacred. If there were any fear as to what my partner and I might really have had to say to each other, I now had a new way to look at the disturbance: that communication was just temporarily blocked because of something I was not seeing—*but what?* This turned the responsibility back on me and ignited my curiosity. *What's in there? What thought just wants to be seen?* Dreading a conversation was no longer a reason to run away in terror and avoid it. Rather, it was a cause to celebrate, get clear, transcend fear, and deepen the love.

In *satsang*, Nick taught a lucid process of conscious communication. In fact, you'll remember the Ivy League heartthrob who referred me to meditation while breaking up with me in Chapter Four. He was utilizing this conscious communication process as he learned it from Nick. And although the message was hard for me to hear on that day, something about the way he communicated with compassion his desire to also date other women did uplift an otherwise depressing conversation and left me with an optimistic feeling that *there are people out there who care for one another.*

Over time, I came to learn the process by applying it in my every spoken (and often unspoken) breath. One day while still living in Costa Rica, I reflected on this blessed art in my journal, because no matter how much I learn about something through someone else's lips, writing about it helps me recognize the wisdom as my own. That's when I dreamed up the acronym **A LETTING**, which Nick and I have used for years when sharing with couples the art of Self-inquiry and conscious communication. May you enjoy it too and make valuable use of it.

• **A is for "Asking."** Conscious communication begins with an earnest, non-projecting question. An example is not "Why did *you* do that?" but "What action or behavior of mine contributed to creating this situation we're both experiencing?" The true asking is not in the words, but in the *feeling* of wanting to understand. The desire to live in harmony with this person is so powerful that you are ready to see the situation through their eyes.

• **L is for "Listening."** Listening is the heart of communication, for if you don't really hear what someone is saying, how can you see things from their perspective? Listening with the intention of perceiving the situation through their eyes is the lifeblood of empathy and compassion. In exchange for this sacred offering of undivided attention, expect to receive insightful information from your partner regarding why a particular situation has manifested in your experience. Remember that they are within you and will, like the Oracle in *The Matrix*, tell you exactly what you most need to hear in that moment. Faith and trust in this process is essential.

• **E is for "Eye Contact."** The quality of eye contact reflects how present you both are during the communication process. If your eyes are wandering, then your mind is wandering; if their stare is vacant, something is blocking connection. In either case, effective communication is not occurring. Your ears might be hearing what they are saying, yet authentic listening is a drinking in of their words and body language through your heart, which is the only access pass to theirs.

As sensitivity is cultivated by practicing this style of communication, you will come to feel deeply at peace while looking into their eyes. You will know definitively that their eye contact is sincere when yours is. If eyes drift, it is appropriate for either partner to request eye contact be maintained (for example: "Please, would you maintain eye contact with me?") and then to follow up with questions to ensure that understanding has transpired (for example: "How would you summarize what I just shared with you?" and "Can you understand why I reacted that way?"). Recognize that it is not a cause for defensiveness but gratitude when this occurs.

• **TT is for "Truth Telling."** For a communication to transform an off-key relationship situation into a harmonious one, the conversation must be rooted in truth. Lies serve only to inflame drama. All human beings, as expressions of the Infinite Intelligence, possess an innate truth detector and can sense when they are being lied to. Whether your partner is telling the truth is not your main concern. The essential question is: *Are you?*

If you are being honest in every area of your life, then they must be, for they are always reflecting you back to yourself 100 percent of the time. Self-honesty is a private, soul-searching matter and is something one can only know within themselves. "But I don't know if I'm being honest" is a common response, to which you may ask yourself, "Do I honestly know if I know this?" This inner-directed acceptance process tunes the innate truth detector, and soon you will know all you need to know.

• **I is for "Inquiry."** Inquiry here is not meant in the sense of asking questions, but in practicing Self-inquiry (i.e., remaining Self-aware throughout the communication). In understanding Self-inquiry, one consciously utilizes the denser sense of "me" to stay aware as Presence: knowing that the light of your consciousness must be turned on, or nothing could ever appear to you. When something your partner communicates evokes a feeling or emotion, the Self-inquiry is an inward investigation of "To whom is this occurring?" Once you feel it is occurring to "me," investigate inwardly:

Who am I?

As your Self-awareness expands via this steady practice, you will eventually find the Self-inquiry to be happening on its own, like a nonphysical vacuum cleaner clearing any mental debris obstructing the path of conscious communication.

• **N is for "Nakedness."** Throughout a conscious communication, both partners must be naked, not physically but in the sense of laying yourself bare as you ask questions and receive your partner's answers. Your task is to remain open and vulnerable, even if it seems your partner is not. Let yourself fully feel any and all emotions that arise in response to what is being said, without reacting or defending your personal position. If you wish to feel the sublimely still presence of love, you must be willing to get hurt, to give up the need to be right, and to surrender any desires to be seen by the other in a positive or particular way. The changeable character you're playing is not the essence of who you are—and at the core of their being, your partner is aware of this act.

The only way to know if your partner is baring it all is to ask yourself, *"Am I?"* Although most believe physical nakedness is a turn-on, you'll find this brand of nakedness, once you strip down all the layers, is the ultimate source of all sensual attraction.

- **G is for "Gratitude."** In my experience, nothing is more attractive than someone who, through their willingness to lay themselves bare to *whatever is so*, opens a portal within me to experience the unconditional acceptance that is true love; and with this arises the inextricable sense of gratitude. When gratitude arises, you'll know this communication is complete. An alive, pulsating sense of oneness may naturally draw you both into a heart-to-heart embrace, at which point it is beautiful to remain silent following the transformative exchange of words, allowing the connection to deepen. Within this abyss of bliss, it is clear: it is not your partner's physical body that is the Source of the love you feel. Your Heart is.

THE GLASS JAR

*O*n the starry summer nights of my childhood, I adored running, jumping, and catching fireflies between my cupped hands, then peeking through the hole formed by my thumbs to watch them illumine neon yellow as they tickled my skin with their itty-bitty feet. Each time I held one, the sensation tingled through my arms and into my heart, activating the reflex to loosen my grip and release the fragile critter back into the night sky. My love affair with lightning bugs lingered until I finally dreamed up a way to keep one of these beloved creatures as a pet.

One day, I tugged at the edge of my mother's muumuu. "Ma, please may I have one of your empty tomato sauce jars? I want to catch a firefly tonight." Since I was always making artwork out of toilet paper rolls, pipe cleaners, and other household treasures, without question she placed it in my open hands and helped me puncture a smattering of breathing holes in its golden twist-on lid.

Not a minute after sunset, I dashed out into the backyard and captured the first specimen in sight, delicately coaxing him into my jar before sealing it tightly. I set the jar upon the patio table and watched the bug fly around my magical panopticon for several minutes, enjoying the private light show I'd cleverly crafted with my own two hands. I even named my new pet "Tomato," in honor of the glass encasement. Yet, it was not long before my mother joined me and asked how I felt about what I'd just done. From our short discussion, I came to understand that if I loved Tomato, I'd have to set him free. After closing my eyes in mindful consideration, I did so hesitantly. But the resistance in my heart morphed into joy.

Fast-forward more than two decades to the moment of this writing, as this childhood lesson rushes back to me in a flash of insight. Only this time, it's not about my relationship with insects but with people—men, to be precise. Reflecting on three relationships with men I daydreamed about marrying (and two of them, I did marry), I recognize I had unconsciously treated these dear men just like Tomato by attempting to encase them in my idyllic romantic construct, a glass jar I'd been spinning for so long, I simply could not see it anymore.

First, my ex-husband. Ah, my first "real adult" relationship: a marriage that could not have started off more "storybook" if Hans Christian Anderson had written it himself. Immediately after my college graduation and twenty-second birthday celebration, a stunning twenty-one-year-old from Europe willingly landed in my jar. We'd met during the fall semester of my senior year while I was a teaching assistant for an English composition class, wherein I crushed instantly on the near-six-foot, chiseled redhead who wore round glasses and was markedly quieter than the other students in the class. It was not until school ended in May that, in the almost empty university parking lot, I slipped him my number, hoping but not believing he would call. Well, he did . . . and five and a half months later our whimsical union was sealed with a marriage ceremony. We lived cozily within my glass jar for about two years until unspoken expectations and the stress of first jobs, after-hours foreign language lessons, and dependence on each other to find our place in this world built to a crescendo of such intensity that we began escaping through the tiny breathing holes; him I'm not sure where to, and me to the office, the therapist, and the gym in desperate attempts to keep myself attractive to him. Three years later, I unscrewed the lid and excused myself from the relationship via a speedy divorce. Still, I was not free of attachment to my idea of "the perfect romance" ... and *plunk*, my fantasy drew me right back into the jar.

The second man I invited in was about eight years older than me, somewhere in his mid-thirties, with the promise of more worldly experiences under his belt. This sharp-talking PR agent from NYC alighted in my jar via my inbox at work. One phone call and I was convinced I wanted only this man in my jar forever.

Before long, he mailed a first-class package to my home address, which I did give him. The parcel contained a teddy bear and a lightly used copy of *The Art of War* by Sun Tzu. One sniff of it practically had me on the next flight from PBI to JFK, but not before knitting him a seven-foot, ribbed, charcoal-gray scarf and hand-hooking him a beige and navy-blue, velvet-backed throw pillow, featuring my own hand-drawn calligraphy design of the Chinese characters for his favorite word, "balance," which evidently I lacked.

Skilled was he at flattering me in all the right ways, but one week spent roaming Central Park near his apartment waiting for him to get off work so we could go out to dinner and have sex in the restaurant bathroom made it clear that he didn't share my definition of romance. A subsequent offer to fly me back to Manhattan to "share myself" with him and his Calvin Klein underwear model friend—which I declined between a gasp and a quiet burst of tears—did not stop me from picking up when his 917 area code lit up the screen. My anxiety about our relationship shattered my jar and he took off. Still, I didn't believe it, assuming everybody, somewhere deep down inside, wanted the same brand of love and romance I did.

For nine months, I rationalized that he just feared commitment and didn't know what he wanted—and I believed that somehow I could *learn him* about "love." This because he often phoned in to the scene of the shards and distracted me from my misery with awkward phone sex and tantalizing talk. So I kept on fumbling in my pile of broken glass until—*aha!*—I discovered the only way out of this mess: glue my jar back together in the loneliest hours of the night. Only this time I would learn to meditate before inviting another man in.

This third effort proved a charm. My relationship with Nick instantaneously "fit" into the glass jar of my dreams, perhaps because at this point, I'd become crystal clear about what I *didn't* want in my jar. He and I lived so ecstatically inside the jar that we explored every cubic millimeter of it together. When not holding hands like children, we were lifting each other up on our shoulders to reach new heights and survey new horizons from Florida to India to Costa Rica and back. We got our fingerprints everywhere while crawling up the sides. We caught each other whenever we slipped along the periphery. Then one day, I made it to the top, peeked out the air holes, and realized there was no more reason to contain our love within the jar. The jar had served its purpose and it was time for us to spread our wings and fly out.

Although I had the urge to fly, I felt terrified. I didn't want to leave this perfect jar! Yet, I was overcome by the beauty of this man as he reflected my own transformation into a liberated being. He flew out first, leaving me alone inside the jar (and inside our cabin in Costa Rica) for two weeks in the summer of 2009 (which was actually the winter there). He'd found a secret place to meditate and asked me to allow him time there alone, and if I would, to leave him fresh water in a designated spot, which I did.

The way his body appeared when he returned to our cabin, it looked like physical death was on the way. I had no choice but to allow the pain, and the futility of grasping the air inside the metaphorical jar, to just be there until I finally found the inner strength to let go and accept that *the destiny of his body will be what it will be.* His body did not perish in this experience. The whole time I'd missed his physical presence, I cried, wrote, lightly slept, and cried some more, comforted only by the divine wisdom of Tomato the Lightning Bug and my mother's words: "If you love him, set him free."

This lesson has been alive in me every day, ever since.

Certainly I recognize that none of these men were "mine" to set free. Yet, in choosing to see them as free and flying off toward their destinies, I now find myself free to do the same, no longer suffering in a glass jar of romantic attachment wherein my love cannot be contained.

Sabotage No More

Whether in the movies or the drama of "real life," nothing used to sadden me more than seeing someone sabotage their chance for love: a woman clicks with a beautiful stranger at a party, but turns down a date because "they're not my type." A guy friend quits the latest dating site after the free trial, convinced "it will never work" when deep down he really just fears rejection. Another friend blessed with a committed relationship gives in to an urge to sleep around and is distraught when their partner moves on. And I would wonder, "*What* were they thinking?" without stopping to question why *I* was feeling the heartache.

It was always easier to point fingers at someone who appeared to be sabotaging their relationship than to confront the "saboteur within." Aspiring to be "the perfect wife," I never, ever wanted to sabotage my relationship. I obsessed over the biblical passage:

> *Who can find a good woman?*
> *She is precious beyond all things.*
> *Her husband's heart trusts her completely.*
> *She is his best reward. (Proverbs 31:10-11)*

This proverb reentered my life in 2004 via the dedication emblazoned on my copy of the *Tao Te Ching* translated by Stephen Mitchell.[17] Early in my *sadhana*, I strived to be that beautiful woman more (cue *The Lord of the Rings*' Sméagol voice) *precious* than rubies to Nick. Yet, my relationship with him was revealing that this idea was not dependent on gender: a good *lover* was turning out to be the priceless thing. Our life together was peeling back my layers of thought to literally reveal my lover as my own precious *Self* (beyond all things)!

How essential this realization turned out to be! All my striving to be acknowledged as a gem of a woman fizzled away and my heart was replenished with gratitude for the opportunity to embody the lover and the Love this proverb is pointing to: that I had given my own self the opportunity to act this drama out, to know harmony with a lover in flesh and bone, to reap this divine blessing. My next question was: *How do I not squander this chance to love and be loved? How do I even handle this glorious benediction so delicate that it knows no words?*

Only formless ecstasy can begin to describe it.

My first shower in this ecstasy happened after my second *satsang* with Nick. Throughout the closing namaste, we gazed into each other's eyes as my senses bathed in pure silence. Suddenly a tiny thought popped, seemingly from some location in the center of my brain, as exciting as the first kernel exploding in a foil pan of Jiffy Pop.

My God, I think he loves me.

Next, I felt a pop in my chest. How to portray the openness of my heart in that moment? What I can attest to was the willingness to be and embody whatever necessary to sustain this connection I felt: this pure sense that life was perfect and always would be, this unconditional love. Initially, it felt like I was soaring high above the lows of life I'd recently suffered: divorce, one-night stands, and dozens of other dating disappointments. Those moments were certainly not this! But how necessary they'd suddenly become, for the illustrious contrast they provided to this sacred stillness, this vast *no-thing* called love.

How did I instinctively know that all my past disappointments were not *it*? How could I possibly have known that something had been "bad," if I'd never known the timeless "good"? What had led to this remembrance? Was it the man, the meditation, or a moment mystically orchestrated beyond my illusions of control?

Suddenly, palpably . . . the man, the meditation, and the moment were inextricable. The man finally appeared in that moment of true meditation because surrender had finally arisen in my heart.

On this day, I was wearing a lotus T-shirt I'd bought during one of my lonesome shopping sprees at Target because I thought it made me look yogic. Little did I realize that my heart was symbolized in that little lotus blossom centered on my chest, peeking through the muck of suffering, destined to bloom no matter what.

In retrospect, it's plain to see. The most important commitment I ever made—beyond marriage—was to know my True Self before anything else, even the romantic relationship I'd spent my whole life convinced I was alive for. In time, the practice of Self-inquiry revealed to me that the heart's default setting is the stillness of pure love.

∞

So back to that willingness I described earlier, the wildly alive willingness to do whatever it takes to sustain the awareness of love. This sense of awareness I felt when I locked eyes with Nick was all I'd ever wanted: the sweet, ineffable assuredness of unconditional love. Now I had everything!

Yet, after a few days together, which can only be described as a virtual honeymoon of uninterrupted joy... "it" showed up.

What do I mean by "it?"

The thought: *I don't want anything to disrupt this bliss.*

Now that everything was finally right, the elusive saboteur had entered stage left.

Soon, like an army of Agent Smiths from *The Matrix*, a slew of actors applying for the part of saboteur manifested in my experience.

First, "it" took the form of my family. No blood relative of mine wanted me dating someone as unfamiliar to them as "a guru" and made their opinions known: by phone, email, voicemail, and once even a deceptive snail-mail parcel marked with Nick's return address, pretending to be from him. Coming face to face with each family member as I stood up for my right to live life on my own terms, I came to understand what Jesus meant when he said that "the members of your own family will be your greatest enemy" (Matthew 10:36) on the path of spiritual awakening.

Second, "it" showed up as the publisher who provided my steady paycheck and the boss to whom I reported. I was still obsessed with dazzling them. Most evenings, I called Nick at 6:15 from the car, confessing I'd stayed late to finish "one more thing." I proceeded to check my email before bed. I found it impossible to leave my work at the office—how could I desert it when it had been so loyal, filling my empty nights with a sense of meaning and purpose? The compulsion to go above and beyond the job description had fueled my world and my bosses had come to expect perfection of me. I had brought it on myself. "She always exceeds her own expectations" had been my mantra since a teacher said that about me at my sixth-grade graduation ceremony. Now I was totally conflicted. All my workaholic tendencies and survival fears were encroaching on my new love space. My brain hurt from writing cover lines for the magazine in my head while smooching with Nick. I quickly noticed these activities could not be performed effectively together. And as presence arose through my meditation practice, I realized these activities could not even be performed at the same time. *What do you mean, I don't have to work all the time to be loved?*

Third, "it" was, frankly, every man on earth. I had to confront my fear of the desires I still felt for—gasp!—"other men." Initially I worried that mere thoughts of past lovers would ruin my new relationship. This OCD anxiety morphed into fear of sighting any man I might desire sexually. That pretty much expanded to include the fear of every man. *Oh my God, what if I was turned on by all of them?! What would that mean about me?* I finally got what my late psych-lit mentor Norm Holland was talking about when he broke down Freud's theories of fear and desire. This idea that *"what you fear, you also desire"* had tailgated just outside my brain for years. Heaven knew, this once-"good Catholic girl" had repressed the desires I was afraid to look at. Whenever I felt a palpable attraction toward anyone who was not Nick, I felt terrible, punishable, and unworthy of love. And *thinking* that my feelings were evil and wrong, I continued to repress my desire all the more … until I witnessed the snowballing nature of desire—and it needed some heat to melt!

Fourth, "it" was my own broken-open heart. Just when I thought I'd escaped the fear and transcended sabotage forever, it came time to own the biggest, relationship-sabotaging projection of all time: forgiving an ex for his unfaithfulness, yes, "the unforgivable."

How to transcend the rage I felt over that cheatin' A?

In this dance of human love, who hasn't seen a relationship end due to unfaithfulness? Yet I've discovered that no matter "who cheated," holding on to any sliver of the unfaithfulness story just sets one up for more of the same suffering. At its core, unfaithfulness is unconsciousness. Not in the "OMG, they are *so* unconscious" judgmental sense, but as a lack of integrity and awareness that this action is sabotaging the sacred relationship or marriage I already have the agreement for. Some may have been conditioned to feel they don't deserve happiness, and so their actions throw water on any spark of love before it's set ablaze. Or sparks fly and the intimacy gets too hot, so they jump into relationships that do not require them to stand naked . . . of their conditioning, that is. Unaware of love's great invitation, people may run in the other direction to familiar parties who reinforce their sense of separate identity: colleagues, coworkers, lovers, mistresses, parents, children, friends, and followers on social media—until they are ready to look in the mirror.

All relationships are a mirror. I have heard many people deny this, yet in my experience it is true, every single time. *A couple's readiness to be in love is a heart resonance, vibrating at the same frequency.* It is impossible that one person jumped in or out of the relationship and the other didn't in some way. No one can be cheated on if they were not, in some way or another, also placing someone or something *before* the love and total acceptance of each other. You may wish to know that I hated acknowledging this at first. Merely considering whether it could be true sent me into a tailspin of denial—and then self-deprecation as I soon recognized its truth via the basic physics of it: for every action, there is an equal and opposite reaction. When my ex had been unfaithful in one way, I had been unfaithful in another. Engaging in fake orgasms, office flirtations, and ill-timed fantasies about the weather man might not be what is traditionally considered infidelity, but I could no longer deny their overarching implication that I'd not been fully present in my relationship. *Could I forgive myself?*

No, not initially.

Could I accept that what had happened . . . had happened?

Yes, though reluctantly at first.

Okay, yes, I could do that much.

And who was I to judge either of us, anyway?

Who was *I,* period?

Therein lay the only solution: the inward quest, posed in all sincerity . . . the proverbial inquiry: *Who am I?* Because how can I have the problem if there is nobody here to have the problem?

This radically simple Self-inquiry, fueled by unwavering acceptance, proved to be the golden ticket. It was the answer to all my questions and the question to all my answers.

One sincere Self-inquiry and the details of the personal story fell like dominoes. Just like that, it all lay before me: my family, my boss, every man on earth, cheating ex . . . all versus Penelope. It had not happened *to* me . . . but *within* me. With that insight, I could love all the players *as* me. As producer of this play titled "My Love Life," I could send the cast, crew, and the extras home and decide whether I wanted any more acts of relationship sabotage. It was a no-brainer.

How perfectly all of the actors play their roles. Yes, even the so-called "villains." None of us has the individual power to extinguish a single spark of love, but memories of our futile attempts shine on as reminders of the Love that has never lied, cheated, or disappeared . . . because this Love is always here.

THE SALTY TASTE OF LOVE

As I mentioned earlier, Nick and I lived in a teensy wooden cabin sequestered within an emerald mountain valley in the cloud forests of Costa Rica. There we awakened to the rush of the river, birdsong, rainbows, and mist glimmering like diamonds across the horizon. When it was not raining, the clear, sunny skies embraced us with the bluest of hues and the blackness of night bathed us in energetic purity, whispering with the glitter of a billion stars. Yet, after nearly three years of residing there, I chose to leave this paradise and move back to the States. As much as I loved its pristine quality, I craved soulful community and human connection. Most people did not, or perhaps could not, stay too long on these consecrated grounds devoid of creature comforts. Nick was an exception. He wanted to stay. I agonized over the decision and yet could not deny the longing to return to the familiar world. And so I left, strengthened by the grace of the woods and a surge of courage I could not otherwise explain.

As the plane hit the runway in South Florida, people I knew and even a stranger I'd befriended during the flight were ready to support the "Penelope, you're so brave, I'm sorry Nick abandoned you" story—and believe me, after years in isolation, I was grateful to receive almost any attention, even if in the form of sympathy. But deep in my bones, I knew that Nick had not abandoned me. I understood, at least on an intellectual level, that my heart was making a choice I did not yet understand.

The nameless pain, which I'd first noticed as I wheeled my suitcase up the rocky path from the cabin, had carved a bottomless cranny in my chest. It lingered for weeks. Relief was nowhere to be found, not even at my tried-and-true sanctuary, the Atlantic Ocean waters of my youth, to which I faithfully returned. The dream of Nick and Penelope, as I'd known it, was over. *Poof!* It had slipped through my fingers like sand through an hourglass and whenever I tried to grab hold of "us" again, my heart felt as if it were being minced into ever-finer grains of this pain. At the peak of the anguish, these words that had burst off my tongue five years earlier returned to me like a message in a bottle: *I don't want it to be over.*

After a few marathon long-distance calls wherein I expressed my heart's wish, Nick returned to Florida and we were back together again. Still, that didn't heal the pain, so clearly was he not its cause or its cure. We rented a condo on the beach and went about our daily activities. I returned to the publishing field. Editing and designing books kept me busy from nine to five and fulfilled my desire for human connection. And as soon as word spread that we were back in town, Tuesday and Friday meditations and *satsang* resumed at our home, along with weekend programs.

During that phase of our lives, Nick's work of disseminating a teaching that turns the mind inward involved countless hours, day and night, spent with his attention turned within to "first person." So maybe I shouldn't have been so surprised when he again was sliding in and out of *samadhi* for weeks at a time. This left me once more with long intervals to silently turn within myself, likewise withdrawing attention from second and third person objects of the world. In my before- and after-work hours, when not meditating or reading conscious books, I journaled and walked the beach, listening to the ebb and flow of the ocean. One particular evening while standing next to a sea turtle nest under the stars, I found myself as alone as I'd felt in the woods, reflecting on where Nick and I were headed together.

Where is he and what good is having a partner if I'm still all alone? I threw up my hands to the sky.

"*Wait . . . who feels alone?*" I asked myself before turning my back toward the sea and heading inside. I tiptoed past Nick, whose attention was still fully absorbed within even as I undressed and climbed into bed. As an editor, I knew my grammar. *Have I seriously been relegated to a second- and third-person object in Nick's dream?*

The next morning, I woke up depressed with no will to get up, get dressed, or stroll the beach. I must have rolled out of bed and sleepwalked because I found myself half-asleep on the toilet when the "Aha!" finally came. After years of fantasizing I would forever be Nick's Snow White, in truth I was more like Humpty Dumpty: totally broken. Even the throne beneath me could not hold me up any longer and I fell forward onto my knees. Nothing could put "me" back together again.

And with that, the wailing started. This was not like any cry I'd known before. It is not possible to see clearly through hysteria. Yet, there is grace when tears gush out through the eyes like water through uncapped hydrants: the world loses its solid appearance.

At this point, with my body hunched over the cold, porcelain tiles, I was teetering on the edge of realization: of knowing—really *knowing*—that the love story I'd been living with this man was not bound by form. That this kind of love was the real deal: eternal.

Endless Love had been my vision since the childhood days when I'd animated my Barbie and Ken dolls toward this auspicious fate to the soundtrack of the matching Lionel Richie-Diana Ross duet, of course. But this was not a practice run on a couple of plastic toys; this was my life! And I so didn't want to fail at love and romance. *Had I confused the two?*

Between sobs, I glimpsed a single bathroom tile illumined by the direct morning sun. It shined so brightly, I had to squint. I literally started to see the light. It occurred to me that I had a choice either to mourn the relationship I was not going to have or celebrate the one I did have right now with someone who loves me as much as Life Itself.

The thought of being loved for What I Truly Am should have been comforting, yet I still yearned for physical affection while Nick was turned inward. *Had I not yet fully surrendered the "I am the body" thought and was I playing the part of a desperate housewife?* Tears and snot soaked my powder-blue baby doll pajamas. *I am still sexy and adorable—and dammit, I want him to want me!*

Then, suddenly, I saw it.

The demand.

That wanting someone I love to want for anything—even me—isn't unconditional Love.

No . . . oh my God! I heard the words within as the choice was re-presented: to cut the strings of attachment, or not.

For as long as I could remember, I'd wanted true love. *Now where was Alex Trebek?* Because God was playing double jeopardy with me, and I didn't know whether to laugh or cry harder. Then, when I chose *love, no-strings-attached love,* my body started to *burn.* An out-of-body experience ensued where I saw it reduced to a whimpering wreck leaning against a toilet bowl . . . and it terrified me.

Am I going to die of a broken heart?

Wait . . . who's saying that?

The Self-inquiry process took over. Suddenly everything "Nick" had taught "me" was happening on automatic pilot. I acknowledged the suffering and looked right at the one who was suffering.

Then came a grand show of emotions with which I had composed my "personal" story. I heard not only a symphony of boundless joy but the cacophony of fears, sadness, disappointment, and resentment that, in spite of their heavy overtones, harmonized in a love song called "Penelope and Nick." I honored every note by allowing each to tickle or sting my soul for a moment, before passing on to the next, and on and on. This time I felt especially grateful to experience each previously dreaded emotion, because in unabashedly witnessing them, I was finally released from their grip.

Throughout this private concert of liberation, my sense of awareness floated skyward, higher and higher, merging into the clear, empty space beyond and within imagination. From there I watched the fragments of my stories, past and future, fall from the clouds and take shape as the cleansing teardrops landing on my feet. The wisdom *as within, so without* awakened in my heart.

When I finally stood up, I peered out the window at the sparkling sea. The sun had risen high above my view. Time had passed but there was nowhere else I had to be. I returned to the bedroom, licking the salty taste of realization off my lips. Without making a sound, I slipped back into the softness of our bed and nestled backwards into Nick's arms. As we spooned, I rested in the remembrance:

I am the Love I always wanted.

Before, during, and after my river of dreams flows into the ocean of life, I am the Love that makes everything possible and all dreams come true.

The End

This sacred story —
yours and mine
passes through
the sands of time,
converging on
a beach
where we
say hello,
beloved friend,
I love you so —
and although
one day
I'll have to go,
let's be
still here
a moment,
burrow our toes
in the earth,
say farewell to death
and rebirth,
and softly kiss
each other's skin
until the ocean
waves us in
for the deep dive
that transcends
The End once
and for all

Afterword:

Embracing the Tantric Journey

or years, readers have asked me how to find a conscious partner and use lovemaking as a meditation or spiritual practice. I also have heard from some who theorized that I just got lucky, their words expressing a sense of hopelessness that Cupid's arrow would ever pierce them, much less deliver to them the perfect Tantra partner on his wings. It is true that I am fortunate. I am filled with gratitude for the blessing of a Self-realized lover, particularly one who constantly reminds me that "like attracts like" and showers me with reminders that the good I see in him is a reflection of my own Heart. But before I recognized him as an outpicturing of it, all I can say is that it was *definitely* my lifelong intention to experience this brand of love and, even while almost drowning in a sea of lust-based relationships, I never stopped believing that true love was possible.

One of the most effective ways to discover a spiritually compatible partner is to show up in places where people are practicing meditation, since Tantra is essentially a form of meditation. The two practices are symbiotically related: meditation stills the mind to relax the body, and Tantra utilizes the body to still the mind. And since people who meditate properly tend to be more sensitive and open-minded, they are generally the ripest for the journey that blends sacred sexuality and Self-knowledge.

In other instances, readers have emailed me expressing curiosity about the sexual aspects of Tantra and in the same breath proclaimed, "But I can't meditate." If you resonate with this camp, in that you don't meditate yet, but are interested in Tantra, then I suggest learning Self-inquiry. Over many years, I have observed that those regularly attending a Self-inquiry *satsang* have increased their resonance for meeting a potential lover who is conscious and open to exploring Tantra. Not that you will necessarily meet them in *satsang*, but practicing Self-inquiry makes one vibrationally relative to attracting those with matching intentions for an authentic spiritual awakening.

If you are meditating regularly, it is relatively easy to introduce another person to the idea of exploring Tantra, assuming that you feel a soul resonance with them and are available to enter into a conscious relationship. Due to the intimate physical and emotional nature of Tantric sexuality, in my experience it works beautifully with a monogamous relationship where both partners can venture deeply into emotions that are stirred up between the two. Whether people want to practice with more than one partner is a karmic matter that one must resolve within. For me, monogamy simplified the data streaming into my inner world from the "outside world" by inviting in only one person's set of conditioning as a contrasting trigger to my own, all of which must be surrendered to ascertain "the Essence," which is, in my view, the whole point of Tantra. Also, it is okay if your mind is still somewhat active despite your efforts to meditate, since Tantra effectively assists with stilling the mind. Even if you don't mention Tantra when you start dating someone, as long as you both continue to meditate regularly, a more sensual and tender relationship that is Tantric in nature is bound to evolve.

If you already have a partner and would like to embark on the Tantric journey, then the importance of becoming meditative applies to both partners. I have observed that the most effective way to introduce your lover to Tantra is by practicing meditation yourself. And if you've never meditated before, you can always learn. Taking instruction in Self-inquiry, either alone or with your partner, is a wonderfully gradual manner in which to begin your Tantric path. In my experience, if Tantra is not coupled with Self-inquiry, the path will begin and end pointing to the "other" partner as your destiny, obscuring the Ultimate Understanding. A deep dive into Self-inquiry—in the form of *"Who am I?"* or *"What am I?"*—leads you to wake up in Love once and forevermore. Being in Love is anchoring your attention in the Heart, which is not a physical place but a state of pure Being wherein identification with the body that meditates and practices Tantra dissolves into oneness, allowing the living of life from pure awareness.

If you feel drawn toward these ideas, but for some reason your partner does not, you can still meditate and even attend classes or *satsang* regularly. Perhaps your partner just needs a little evidence of the benefits of meditation before he or she is willing to try it and reap its blessings. And who better to introduce these gifts than you? Patience with your practice, and your partner, is everything. I would gently invite them but not push it, as that may squash any chance of them eventually becoming receptive to the idea.

Allowing is the greatest demonstration of love.

And it always begins with you living it.

ACKNOWLEDGMENTS

*W*hat is a book if not a tapestry of gratitude? In the case of *Wake Up in Love*, I have these delightful friends to thank: my co-creators in spinning this love story into a book to have and to hold: Jaime Cox, Meryl Davids Landau, T.G. Monahan, Abby Murphy, and Jordan Turchek, for their wise and wonderful editing.

My first mentors in publishing: Dr. Phillip Lucas, for imparting the wisdom of the editing craft and for showing up as conscious company long before I knew what it was; Professor Mindy McAdams, for carrying forward the torch of journalistic ideals from print into digital realms and for inspiring me to write using technologies that dissolve all boundaries between the world and the elegant Source code beneath; and Dr. Kim Walsh-Childers, for teaching me the art of investigative reporting and impressing upon my heart the living, breathing definition of *dignity:* that everybody has a story worth uncovering. And that it comes to light by asking questions and listening with care, sensitivity, and devotion to the truth. This trio inspired me to pursue writing and publishing as a vocation—what a perfect way to love, serve, and remember who I am.

The authors I have worked with over the years: every single one has held up a clear mirror reflecting facets of life I needed to understand. I cherish each of our relationships and would not have wished to learn these lessons any other way.

The original publisher of my *Love Life* column, Raven Solsong. *Montaña al Mar* proved much more than a magazine for those of us residing in southern Costa Rica between 2008 and 2010. I remain grateful to the readers who responded to my articles with inner reflection, emails, and hugs when serendipity drew us together like magnets on those days that I would trek for two hours down the mountain to sit in cafés and resuscitate my social life.

The publisher of my earliest essays and first Facebook friend, Dave Fine, for his encouragement to the tune of "if you write enough essays, one morning you will wake up and realize that you have written a book."

Our Costa Rican landlords Peter and Paqui, for letting us live in a heaven on earth, a place that made it possible to unmistakably attune to and record the inner voice of wisdom in sacred quietude.

The Self-Inquiry Center family, for your enduring love and friendship.

My friend Rebecca Fedele, who for nearly a decade straight and from all corners of the globe, provoked me with shrugging emojis to finish this book.

Teachers Jesus of Nazareth, Sri Ramana Maharshi, Osho, Sri Sadhu Om Swamigal, Anandamayi Ma, Vasistha, Mikhail Naimy, and Hafiz, for tilling the soil of the Heart and planting the seeds of Love, Self-inquiry, and Grace, revealing the truth that shines clear.

Liebchen the Pomeranian, exquisite guardian of being, for taking me out for walks and keeping my back warm at night.

And Nick Gancitano, my beloved husband, for everything.

The Flight Beyond

Thank You for falling with me

so we could tumble and climb

in breathless discovery

of the flight beyond mind

and hold inner sight

of the Love that's not blind

but deeply aware,

ever there

breathing us,

leading us

one step

at

a

t

i

m

e

ENDNOTES

1. Berdon, Eileen. "D.H. Lawrence Biography." *Internet Movie Database.* Accessed May 31, 2020. https://www.imdb.com/name/nm0492692/bio.

2. Arntz, William, Chasse, Betsy, Guzze, Todd C., and Vicente, Mark. (Producers), and Arntz, William, Chasse, Betsy, and Vicente, Mark. (Director). (2005) *What the Bleep Do We Know?* [Documentary film] United States: Captured Light and Lord of the Wind Films, LLC.

3. Treya Killam Wilber quotes are sourced from the second edition of Ken Wilber's *Grace and Grit: Spirituality and Healing in the Life and Death of Treya Killam Wilber* (Shambhala, 2001), pages 239-241.

4. Emoto, Masaru. *The Hidden Messages in Water* (Atria Books, 2005).

5. Stein, Joel. "Just Say Om." *Time* 162, no. 5. (2003): 48-52. Accessed June 4, 2020. http://content.time.com/time/magazine/article/0,9171,1005349,00.html. Cover image is viewable at http://content.time.com/time/covers/0,16641,20030804,00.html.

6. Maharshi, Sri Ramana. "Death Experience." Sri Ramana sramam. Accessed May 31, 2020. https://www.sriramanamaharshi.org/ramana-maharshi/death-experience/.

7. Ibid.

8. Maharshi, Sri Ramana. *The Spiritual Teachings of Ramana Maharshi.* (Shambhala Press, 2004).

9. Jung, Carl. "Sri Ramana and His Message to Modern Man." Foreword to *The Spiritual Teaching of Ramana Maharshi.* (Shambhala Press, 2004), ix.

10. Ibid, xii.

11. Variations of this quote are attributed to Albert Einstein. *Wikiquote.* Accessed December 11, 2020. https://en.wiki quote.org/wiki/Talk:Albert_Einstein.

12. Mitchell, Stephen. *The Gospel According to Jesus: A New Translation and Guide to His Essential Teachings for Believers and Unbelievers.* (Harper Perennial, 1994).

13. Sengupta, Jayita. *Feminist Perspectives in the Novels of Toni Morrison, Michèle Roberts and Anita Desai.* (New Delhi: Atlantic Publishing India, 2006).

14. Excerpted from the description on the Oxford World's Classics edition of the *Vatsyayana Kamasutra.* (OUP, 2009).

15. Vatsyayana, Doniger, Wendy, and Kakar, Sudhir. *Kamasutra: A New, Complete English Translation of the Sanskrit Text: With excerpts from the Sanskrit Jayamangala commentary of Yashodhara Indrapada, the Hindi Jaya commentary of Devadatta Shastri.* (Oxford: Oxford University Press, 2009), 57.

16. Freud, Sigmund. "Difficulties of Psychoanalysis." In *Character and Culture.* (New York: Collier Books, Div. of Crowell-Collier Publ. Co., 1963), 189.

17. Laozi and Mitchell, Stephen. *Tao Te Ching: A New English Version* [Pocket Edition]. (HarperPerennial, 1992).

ABOUT THE AUTHOR

*P*enelope Love, MA, is a writer, speaker, and poet residing with her husband, Nick Gancitano, in the mountains of North Carolina. Together they share the message of *Wake Up in Love* with those on the blended path of Tantra and Self-inquiry. Their conscious communication workshops and Tantra lectures inspire the heart with a visionary paradigm of awakened partnership.

www.PenelopeLove.com

PUBLISHER'S NOTE

*T*hank you for the opportunity to serve you. If you would like to help share this message, here are some popular ways:

- **Reviews:** Write an online review; in social media posts, tag #wakeupinlovebook

- **Giving:** Gift this book to friends, family, and colleagues

- **Book Clubs:** Request the Reading Group Guide and an author appearance: BookClubs@WakeUpInLove.com

- **Book Tour:** Suggest your city or hometown as a stop: BookTour@WakeUpInLove.com

- **Speaking:** Invite Penelope Love to speak with your organization

- **Workshops:** Organize a Self-inquiry/Tantra workshop in your area: Workshops@WakeUpInLove.com

- **Bulk Orders:** Email Sales@OpenHeartPublishing.com

- **Contact Information:** +1-828-237-2555

We appreciate your book reviews, letters, and shares.

Open Heart
PUBLISHING